Troops
in
Strikes

Military Intervention in
Industrial Disputes

STEVE PEAK

The Cobden Trust

The Cobden Trust
21 Tabard Street
London SE1 4LA

ISBN 0 900137 22 3
PRINTED IN GREAT BRITAIN
by the Russell Press, Nottingham

Contents

PART II: SURVEY OF MILITARY INTERVENTION IN INDUSTRIAL DISPUTES

Illustrations

Military Intervention in Industrial Disputes 1945-1983

1945	Dockers (July)
	Dockers (October)
1946	Smithfield Porters
	Dockers (Southampton)
1947	Road Transport Workers (including Smithfield)
	Dockers
	Tower Bridge Operators
1948	Buckingham Palace Boiler Room Workers
	Dockers *SoE
1949	Dockers *SoE
	Power Station Manual Workers (London)
1950	Dockers
	Smithfield/Road Haulage Drivers
	Gas Maintenance Workers (London)
1953	Oil Tanker Drivers
1955	Railway Footplate Workers *SoE
1960	Seamen
1966	Seamen *SoE
1970	Refuse Collectors (Tower Hamlets)
	Power Station Manual Workers *SoE
1972	Dockers *SoE
1973	Firemen (Glasgow)
1975	Refuse Collectors (Glasgow)
1977	Air Traffic Control Assistants
	Firemen
1978	Naval Dockyard Workers
1979	Ambulance Crews
	Westminster Hospital Ancillary Workers
	Naval Dockyard Workers
	Industrial Civil Servants
1980	Prison Officers
1981	Naval Dockyard Workers
	Ambulance Crews
1982	Ambulance Crews
	Railway Workers
1983	Royal Navy piracy

(Note: *SoE indicates that a state of emergency under the Emergency Powers Act 1920 was declared.)

Acknowledgements

This book is the result of a collaborative project set up by the Cobden Trust and the State Research group. My thanks are due to all the trade unionists, journalists, civil servants, service personnel, politicians and academics who gave information and advice, especially Tony Bradley, Jim Caughlin, Jack Dash, Peter Hennessy, Derek Knight, Gillian Morris, Peter Wallington and the members of the Fire Brigades Union at Bethnal Green Fire Station. I am particularly grateful to Ian Cobain for his invaluable research assistance and to Tony Bunyan for his help.

The Cobden Trust is very grateful to the Joseph Rowntree Charitable Trust and the Cheney Peace Settlement for their financial support for this research without which it could not have been undertaken.

Introduction

'The merits or demerits of [trade] disputes or [industrial] unrest are of no concern whatsoever to soldiers.'[1]

'Give me the chance to go and pick up Mr Michael McGahey and if it turns out to be my last assignment in the army I should die happy.'[2]

British troops have been used by the government in no less than 36 industrial disputes since 1945. In certain industries, the use of troops, or a well publicised threat that they may be used, has become a regular response to strikes. These industries, the majority in the public sector, are those considered crucial to the smooth running of the economy: electricity, gas, oil, water, food distribution, docks, communications, health services, parts of the road haulage industry, and the civilian-operated sections of the military. When considering strike action, the workers in these sectors are now faced with an employer able to summon directly (or indirectly, through the government, in the case of the private sector) a tightly controlled, flexible replacement labour force: the personnel of Britain's three armed services. The complete substitution of troops for the striking Fire Brigade Union members in 1977 shows just how sophisticated and successful the government's strike-breaking apparatus has become.

Strike-breaking troops have been unarmed since 1945 and are not used to threaten or attack the strikers. Their role is to take over the work of the strikers; any public order problems are handled by the police. This was not, however, always the case.

Troops have been used to intervene in strikes since at least the 18th century. This was sometimes as 'blackleg'* labour but more often to display or use force, strikes frequently being accompanied by disturbances. Indeed, until the 1920s the army were often called in to help the police who were unable to keep the peace unaided. (This role is now known as MACP, Military Aid to the Civil Power). It was during the 1926 General Strike that the police

*The term blackleg is usually used to denote a worker who performs the work of a striking worker and is here used to refer to services personnel who perform the same role.

proved themselves both loyal and efficient enough to take over full responsibility for public order, the army retreating into the background to act only as the last defence against insurrection.

From that time on, the army's role in strikes has been that of an unarmed, reserve labour force, providing what is called MACM — Military Aid to the Civil Ministries. The military is used for strike intervention rather than a civilian organisation, primarily because it is both available and can do the job — being a large body of disciplined and fit people, already under state direction, used to receiving orders, historically experienced in the role and relatively isolated from trade unionism. It is also very adaptable:

'The military is by definition a crisis organisation. It has the resources available to enable it to respond quickly and effectively to emergencies and it can improvise much more readily than many of its civilian counterparts.'[3]

The increasing use of the troops to break, or ameliorate the effects of, strikes is significant. Yet it has happened almost without public comment, or opposition from those who are most affected, trade unionists. This is all the more surprising since the legality of this use of the military to intervene in an internal, civil dispute, is highly questionable.

The legal position is complex and is examined closely in chapter two. Whether the government has the power which it claims to use troops to intervene in such disputes remains unresolved. But a strong case can be made that governments acted illegally when they sent in the troops on some, if not the majority of, occasions since the Second World War. On many of these occasions the orders given to the troops may not have been lawful, in which case soldiers could have refused, and could in the future refuse, to obey them. An examination of the historical record, compared with current statements from the Ministry of Defence, reveals that successive governments have themselves been unclear about the legal position and have made contradictory statements justifying their action.

Just as important as the issue of the legality of military intervention is the lack of democratic control over it. Where a declaration of a state of emergency under the Emergency Powers Act 1920 precedes the use of troops, parliament has certain rights — albeit minor — of scrutiny and veto over the very wide authority that governments can take. Governments now strive not to declare states of emergency, however, and in the procedures utilised today parliament has no role, and it can provide no check on the exercise by ministers and officials of the powers they believe they have to deploy troops at will inside Britain.

The more frequent mobilisation of the armed forces to intervene in strikes has followed the changing nature of the state and the economy during the 20th century. The economy has increasingly become centrally managed, and complexly interrelated and thus dependent on the smooth functioning of its main components; it is therefore far more vulnerable to industrial action by even small groups of workers.

If a strike occurs in an 'essential' industry the government needs to break it: first, in order to ensure the continued smooth functioning of the economy and, second, because the public holds the government responsible for ensuring the continued supply of the essentials of life. The state has increasingly had a third motive for breaking strikes in the public sector, however: enforcing government income policies.

The fine line between using troops to maintain essential services, or to enforce income policies, and the blurring of this line by government emphasis only on the former, is a further cause for concern. As Jeffery and Hennessy note in their book on contingency planning: 'Whether or not this [defence of incomes policy] is a justifiable use of emergency powers is open to question'.[4]

The effect of the military's strike-breaking operations on the outcome of each dispute is necessarily immeasurable but undoubtedly, in some cases, considerable. Moreover, by limiting the effectiveness of action challenging government income policies, it has had some impact on the direction of industrial relations and the economy. Why then is the union response so muted?

Until the 1920s the unions did strongly oppose any military intervention in strikes, and the appearance of troops in a industrial dispute was almost guaranteed to exacerbate it. For two reasons this opposition has waned.

The historic opposition to troops ceased, first in the immediate post-war period, when the 1945-51 Labour government used the military in strikes and the trade union leadership with whom it was working closely, acquiesced. The striking workers, in turn, while objecting in principle, showed little personal hostility to the conscripts waiting to be demobilised, whom they regarded as 'workers in uniform'.

Secondly, union response appears to be equivocal because the troops are used 'to maintain essential services', placing the strikers in a difficult ethical and social position. While any amelioration of the effects of strike action reduces their industrial strength, if they prevent troops maintaining essential services they may place the lives of the public in jeopardy — an action for which they will take the blame, however culpable the management may be. An opinion poll in February 1979 at the height of the 'Winter of Discontent' showed that 78 per cent of the public were in favour of the use of troops in key industries, with 71 per cent of trade unionists supporting this as well.[5]

Knowing when and how to oppose military intervention in strikes is therefore a difficult moral and practical problem for the unions. Governments have, not surprisingly, emphasised the 'essential services' role of the troops and insisted on their neutrality in the dispute itself. As long ago as 1911 Winston Churchill insisted that there was no question of using troops to intervene in a labour dispute itself and a secret report prepared by Lord Carrington in 1977 makes it quite clear that governments recognise the necessity of winning public support for the use of troops with effective propaganda.[6]

The approach taken by the Ministry of Defence and by the military themselves indicates their sensitivity to the need to legitimise their strike-breaking role. While the MoD presents each incident of strike-breaking as a temporary, atypical event, the army ensures that the troops do not identify with the interests of the trade unionists, for the government's ability to use the forces depends on their willingness to perform tasks which are far removed from the pictures in the recruiting brochures.

Rigid military discipline usually ensures compliance with superior orders but class and nationalities are recognised by the military authorities as being potentially stronger. An anonymous infantry battalion commanding officer summarised their problems during the 1973-4 miners strike: 'If we were engaged in shifting supplies for weeks on end and there was large-scale workers' hostility to our doing it, I think that at the very least one would get restlessness among the chaps. Of course, a lot would depend on how the matter was handled — you don't send Welsh units to do the job in Cardiff any more than you send Irish units to Ulster now. It puts their loyalty under too great a strain'.[7]

A former soldier who was put in a military prison for refusing to take part in the breaking of the 1975 Glasgow refuse collectors strike (see page 126) later explained how army officers try to turn ordinary soldiers away from trade unionism:

'I'd be the last person to pretend it's easy to organise as a trade unionist inside the Army. There is a constant barrage of propaganda, through film shows and officers' talks, about greedy workers, communists and trade unions having too much power. But if a start isn't made soon to organise trade union ideas in the Army then soldiers, usually unemployed lads from a working class background like myself, will find themselves being used more and more as strike-breakers, preventing ordinary workers from winning a decent standard of living'.[8]

If propaganda is the state's first means of ensuring support, secrecy is the second. Both the development of the contingency planning apparatus and the actual use of troops have been shrouded in secrecy. Ten years after the Civil Contingencies Unit, where the operations are planned, was set up, its existence was still being officially denied by the government.

This level of secrecy has made research into this area extraordinarily difficult. Details of the planning machinery and of how and when troops have been used are not recorded in any official publications, except in summary in recent annual Statements on the Defence Estimates. The fact that 36 post-1945 instances can be recorded here owes more to newspaper archives and radical pamphlets than to Ministry of Defence records or replies to MPs' parliamentary questions which we have found misleading or inaccurate.

The 1977 national fire brigade strike was a turning point in both the history of military strike-breaking and in the extension of military involvement into British civilian life. During the strike, the military for the first time proved themselves capable of both replacing a complete labour force and of running an industry for a prolonged period without arousing serious public hostility. The success of this operation gave government contingency planners the confidence to extend substantially the scope of their plans for using troops, so that strikes in essential services and industries are now automatically paralleled by contingency plans that ultimately involve military intervention. It appears that there is now a danger that the threat to use troops in the increasing number of 'essential' industries may become a substitute for the negotiation that previously may have taken place to settle these disputes.

Nevertheless, successive governments have played down the extent of their use and prevented public debate about their machinery or plans by keeping the information secret. Government statements about the legal basis of their power to use troops have been inconsistent and its legality is questionable. The decisions to use troops are taken by ministers and officials, parliament increasingly being by-passed, avoiding the publicity and controversy of a public debate.

In this contentious area of government policy, many civil liberty principles are thus at stake: the side-stepping of the democratic process, government secrecy, the legality of the use of troops against the civilian population and the implications for the right of employees to withdraw their labour. Yet almost no research has been done to examine the extent of this practice and the issues behind it. For these reasons the Cobden Trust decided to initiate such a project, based on a survey of each incidence of the use of troops in industrial disputes since 1945. This book is the outcome of that research. It shows that military intervention in civilian strikes is a more extensive practice than had hitherto been realised; that the power to direct it lies almost entirely with a few government ministers and their advisers, and that the law surrounding it is confused and open to challenge.

Chapter one looks at the early history of the use of troops in industrial disputes and the passing of the Emergency Powers Act in 1920, which remains in force today. It discusses the changed role of the troops from one of maintaining order to that of a replacement workforce.

Chapter two examines the development, first, of the law from the 1939 Regulation introduced to deal with war-time conditions to the situation today, showing how the law has been re-interpreted by successive governments and increasingly used to by-pass Parliament. It concludes that in several areas the law is at variance with government practice. Secondly it examines the machinery of contingency planning which first identifies damaging strikes and then takes action against them. The industrial capacity of the military is discussed, showing how many and what sort of troops are available to intervene.

Chapter three begins the survey of strikes in which troops have been used, or their use has been threatened, dealing with the period 1945-70. Chapter four covers 1970-74 and chapter five the period from 1974 to the general election in June 1983. The final chapter summarises the findings and conclusions to be drawn from them and urges that attention be given to the key issue: when is it legitimate for the government to use troops to undermine the effectiveness of industrial action?

This book covers only England, Scotland and Wales. Northern Ireland is excluded because although the legal situation there is broadly similar to that in Britain, the political, social and historical differences justify a detailed study that if included here could easily have doubled the length of this work.

References
1. Manual of Military Law, ninth edition, Part II (1968), p.503.
2. Infantry Battalion commanding officer, on the leader of the Scottish Mineworkers, during the 1973-4 miners strike. Quoted in the *Evening Standard*, 1 February 1974.
3. Gwyn Harries-Jenkins, 'The Collapse of the Imperial Role', in *Perspectives upon British Defence Policy 1945-70* (Southampton University, 1978), p.31.
4. Keith Jeffery and Peter Hennessy, *States of Emergency* (1983), p.266.
5. *The Times*, 26 November 1979.
6. See Jeffery and Hennessy, *op.cit.,* p.255.
7. *Evening Standard*, 1 February 1974.
8. *Socialist Worker*, 26 November 1977.

Part I
CONTINGENCY PLANNING

One

Early History and the Emergency Powers Act 1920

'In times of grave emergency, normal constitutional principles may have to give way to the overriding need to deal with the emergency'.[1]

'Constitutional laws reflect what politicians can get away with'.[2]

The early history of military involvement in strikes is an important one, for on many occasions it was the story of the state's last lines of defence against the chaos that might have resulted from the actions of militant sections of the working class. Without the intervention of troops, many pre-General Strike industrial disputes could, if they had succeeded, have become much wider confrontations between the government and the governed. Since the First World War, the elements of the British economy have become so interdependent that a dispute in one area can cause widespread disruption in the rest of society. It is perhaps not surprising, therefore, that, when faced with fundamental challenges to its authority, the state should sometimes react in extreme ways, even going so far as bending, or even breaking, its own laws if the immediate needs dictated it.

In order to explain both the present law relating to military strike breaking and to put into context the 1945-83 survey of blacklegging operations in chapter three to chapter six, it is necessary, first, to survey the nature of the conflict in the 19th and early 20th centuries. By following some of the snake-like contortions performed with the law, constitution and administrative machinery by successive governments we may come to understand why today's governments attach so much importance to their ability to use troops unilaterally and why they resist any moves to have this power discussed or circumscribed by parliament.

Military intervention in strikes is far from new. What is different today is the use of troops to replace striking workers as one part of government policy for dealing with strikes in certain essential industries.

In the 18th and 19th centuries, before the development of the modern police force, military intervention in the numerous strikes of the time was principally in a public order role, troops being called on to put down the riots which often originated in industrial disputes. After the defeat of the Chartist movement (which sought radical political and industrial change) in the late 1840s, strikes became less political and riotous in character and new police forces began to take over the protection of property and the maintenance of public order. The military were occasionally used as a substitute labour force but more often to back up the police with a show of force until the 1890s. In this relatively peaceful mid-Victorian period, which saw the emergence of the non-militant 'New Model' craft unions of skilled workers, the trade union movement had some success in protesting peacefully against the use of troops in the building trade and on the land.[3]

The early dawn of the modern age of military strike-breaking came with the passing of the Conspiracy and Protection of Property Act 1875 which, amongst its provisions, effectively made it illegal for workers in the gas and water industries to strike. Thereby it signalled the state's first concern that certain industries were 'essential' to the nation, a concept that was to mushroom in the 20th century. Soon after, the development of more aggressive unions for semi-skilled and unskilled workers in the late 1880s gave the first indications of how effective organised trade union action could be, a situation highlighted by the 1889 London dock strike.

With Britain hit by economic depression in the last quarter of the 19th century, strike action became more common and troops were called out on two notable occasions. The first was the 1893 strike of the dockers and seamen in Hull, when cavalry protected the civilian blacklegs who undermined the strike and two gunboats sailed up the Humber. The second strike, five months later, was to become a landmark in trade union and military history and in the development of the modern relationship between civil and military power. During a lockout at the Ackton Hall Colliery at Featherstone in Yorkshire, miners began protesting against the use of blacklegs to move coal. As most of the local police force were 'protecting the pockets of the rich' at Doncaster Races, troops were summoned instead to keep order. This inflamed the miners to such an extent that, in order to prevent the colliery being burnt to the ground, panic-stricken local magistrates ordered the troops to open fire on the crowd. Two innocent bystanders, one a Sunday-school teacher, were killed and several more injured.[4]

The requisitioning of troops for Featherstone had led directly to one of the worst disturbances in Britain for many years and highlighted what was to become a major issue in the series of strikes just before the First World War: could modern governments afford to leave their national law and order/anti-strike policies in the hands of the often incompetent and biased magistrates who, until then, had had the sole legal power to call for troops? By 1914 successive governments had decided that the traditional system was unworkable. One of the arguments of this study, however, is that this traditional position in which the magistrates are responsible for calling out the troops may still be constitutionally correct as their common law powers have not been clearly removed by any government.

Summoning the troops

During the 19th century, the only people who could summon troops to help put down a disturbance (and disturbances were taken to include strikes) were the local magistrates, except in the most dire emergency when, it could be argued, there was a common law duty on the local military officers to intervene on their own initiative. It was the local magistrate who monitored local developments and, at the appropriate moment, was expected to ask for troops.

This system has its origins in the centuries-old British hostility to any standing army controlled by the monarch or government and in the historical role of magistrates as combined judiciary, police, local administrators and agents of central government.

Throughout its early history, the use of the British standing army for operations against the civilian population was fiercely resisted and its legality questioned. Working-class hostility to any form of military intervention in civilian life only begins to diminish after the end of the Second World War.

In the 18th century, the army 'was regarded with deep suspicion by the public. . . Attempts to increase it in size were jealously curtailed, as tending towards setting up military government. . . it remained socially isolated and apologetic about its very existence'.[5] Nevertheless the widespread insurrectionary disorders that lasted through the 18th century and up to the 1840s had to be suppressed and, in the absence of an adequate police force, the body responsible for doing so had to be the military.[6] Public hostility would not allow any overt central government or Crown direction of the armed forces and this, combined with poor communications with the towns and districts of Britain, necessitated a locally-based military mobilisation system. The responsibility fell, naturally, onto the shoulders of the magistrates.

The office of magistrate, or Justice of the Peace, dates from the 14th century and, until the development of modern local government in the 19th century, the magistrates were the 'pivot of all government in the locality'.[7] They held the primary responsibility for maintaining law and order, administering justice and overseeing governmental functions such as the poor law system. During the 19th century, the governmental duties were largely taken away from them but they remain today a powerful and potent institution, appointed from the localities by the government in a curiously British amalgam of central direction and local autonomy of politics and law.

In the 19th century, magistrates were men of property and hence fundamentally opposed to the interests of trade unionists who were often their employees. In the countryside, the rural magistrates were not the aristocracy but the layer of society below them, broadly equivalent to the squirearchy, particularly the larger farmers. In the towns, where most of the militant working class were to be found, the magistrates lacked the 'natural' elevated class position of their rural counterparts, often being shopkeepers and small traders, 'the last people likely to be able to bring their personal authority to bear on rioting workers'.[8]

Despite being, in many cases, the employers of the people they were trying to control, the ancient history of their office and their sensitivity to local issues gave the magistrates a popularly accepted legitimacy, however small, that no other body could command.

The magistrates, as the traditional upholders of law and order, were, therefore, also the officials historically entrusted with the responsibility of deciding when all other methods of riot control had failed and hence when the military needed to be summoned. In the absence of any statute law to the contrary, their position in this respect became part of common law, that non-codified but nonetheless enforceable body of the law that has its origins in the Middle Ages.

For the first decades of the standing army's existence, the monarch, as head of the army, tried to insist that troops could only be used in disturbances after permission had been granted from the crown or government, but this proved to be unworkable and also contrary to the common law if long delays in sending troops were experienced. The requisitioning procedure based on the magistrates was therefore introduced about 1720 and took a roughly similar form to that which continued into the 19th century in 1760. *The Queen's Regulations for the Army* (the army's internal guide to the law) for 1844 set out what was commonly understood by all parties during most of the 19th century to be the common law position regarding the use of troops in Britain in both riots and strikes: 'No Officer is to go out with Troops in the suppression of Riot, the maintenance of the Public Peace, and the execution of the law, except under the requisition of a Magistrate, in writing'.[9] Officers were also not to give the order to open fire 'unless distinctly required to do so by the Magistrate'.[10]

These provisions are based on the fundamental common law principle that 'every citizen is bound to come to the assistance of the civil authority when the civil authority requires his assistance to enforce law and order'.[11] By the late 19th century, the requisitioning body had become known as the 'civil authority' or 'civil power', but this was still taken to refer to the magistrates.

Featherstone's Effects

The unnecessary deaths at Featherstone Colliery in 1893 revealed just how inefficient the traditional system for peace keeping and strike-breaking could be. Moreover, if the system could not even cope with a minor disturbance in one area, how would the country fare during the national strikes that were then becoming a possibility?

This problem was recognised by the government and, following the setting up of, first, in 1893 a Committee of Inquiry into the riot and then in 1894 a Departmental Committee to examine the regulations for calling out the military, changes were made in 1895 in the administrative mobilisation procedure — but *not* the law.

The Departmental Committee worked out a procedure to prevent unnecessary applications for military aid from magistrates. In the boroughs, all requisitions for troops were to go through the mayor (the chief magistrate) and, in the counties, the Chief Constable. In theory, the Chief Constable could only pass the request on to the military but in practice he vetted the application. Indeed, the Select Committee on the Employment of the Military in Cases of Disturbances was told in 1908 that this measure was designed to give the Chief Constable power 'over and above the magistrate'.[12] Magistrates were still expected to attend the disturbance with the military but could no longer give the order to open fire. Instead, they were to order the commanding officer to 'take action' and it was up to the officer to decide what measures to adopt. These changes in procedure were incorporated in the Queen's Regulations in 1895 and thereby became the 'rules' for the military. But they in no way affected the legal position, as the Queen's Regulations have no standing in law.

The government's changes in the 1895 Regulations effectively removed much of the former power of the magistrates, especially in the counties, and began to centralise part of a system which had previously been widely dispersed.

The government did not consider it was breaking the law by issuing administrative orders to the military that appeared to contradict the law. Richard Haldane, Secretary of State for War, told the 1908 Committee: 'They [the Regulations] do not, and cannot, alter the common law. They are mere instructions to the commanding officers and the troops how to behave themselves'.[13]

But this statement conflicts with the reality: the new Regulations effectively made the Chief Constables the 'civil authorities' in the rural areas. Rather than make a controversial amendment to the law, the government bent it by administrative fiat.

Further steps along this road were taken when the 1908 Select Committee recommended strengthening the police forces mutual support schemes, thereby decreasing the need for military assistance. Nearly all of the evidence to the Committee pointed clearly to the undesirability of using troops in disturbances; wherever possible it was argued, the police should be the first and last line of defence. (The Committee had its origins in parliamentary motions put by Labour MPs stating that the powers of the magistrates to summon troops in industrial disputes were open to grave abuses, with riots often ensuing from the mere presence of the military.)

The Committee restated what are still considered to be the principles of military aid to the Civil Authorities: 'That every citizen is bound to assist the Civil Authority in repressing disorder when called upon to do so, an obligation which admits of no distinction as between civil and military status. That for such purposes of repression or suppression no more force than is necessary can lawfully be used. . . . The Civil Authority is responsible for the preservation of the peace, and must therefore take all possible precautions to provide the means of discharging that duty effectively with the forces primarily at its disposal, these being the Police Forces. Thus it is all-important that the Civil Forces should be so organised and administered as to obviate to the utmost possible extent any necessity for resorting to military aid.'[14]

Implicit in the report are the assumptions that 'disturbances' and 'disorder' included strikes and that the 'civil authority' was generally the magistrate.

The Use of Force

The 1908 Committee also considered how much force could be used by the government to quell civil disturbances. Troops have not been used in strikes either to display or use force to any significant extent since the 1920s and the extent to which it could lawfully be used has not, therefore, been a live issue in recent years. With the increasing social upheavals of the 1980s however, it is by no means impossible that troops will once again be needed to quell public disorder. This section briefly reviews how much force they could use were this to occur.

In the House of Commons debate that preceded the setting up of the 1908 Committee, the Secretary of State for War, Richard Haldane, had also said: 'they [the magistrates — 'whose duty it was to restore order'] had no right to call in the military in a case where the police could quell any riot; no right to use firearms where firearms were not necessary, and anyone doing so and killing was guilty of manslaughter.'[15]

Haldane told the Committee: 'The soldier is in no different position from anybody else. He must obey the civil authority by coming to its assistance, where it is necessary that the soldier should give assistance to the civil authority, but it must be necessary that he should do so, and an excess of force and an excess of display ought not to be used. The soldier is guilty of an offence if he uses that excess, even under the direction of the civil authority.'[16]

The current legal position is much the same. The only major change in the relevant law has been the passing of the Criminal Law Act 1967 which simply added to the confusion by saying: 'A person may use such force as is reasonable in the circumstances in the prevention of crime, or in effecting or assisting in the lawful arrest of offenders or suspected offenders or of persons unlawfully at large.'[17] But what is reasonable? No definition is given. As Smith and Hogan say: 'The whole question is somewhat speculative . . . It seems that the question . . . is always for the jury and never a point of law for the judge.'[18] Smith and Hogan go on to suggest that it can very rarely be justifiable to use deadly force merely in the defence of property.[19] *The Manual of Military Law,* however, believes that juries would quite possibly take a sympathetic view of soldiers shooting offenders against property.[20]

An Edwardian Snapshot

The 1908 Committee resulted in some small improvements in the procedure for handling disturbances and briefly focused the government's mind on a problem that was to become a nightmare for it between 1910 and 1914, when a series of bloody confrontations with trade unionists almost culminated in Britain's first general strike.

What did the government's strike-breaking capability look like after the 1908 Committee report at what, in retrospect, can be seen to be the beginning of a new kind of industrial conflict?

The law appeared to be relatively clear, having just been restated by the Committee: the government could not act unilaterally against strikers because, according to the traditional common law, it could only use troops in strikes if the 'civil authority' (generally accepted to be the magistrates) had first requested them. This interpretation of the law was based on the understanding that strikes were common law breaches of the peace, or disturbances.

Whether this was the actual legal position or a very widespread, popular misunderstanding of it is now very difficult to establish. Did nearly two centuries of the magistrates being the 'civil authority' in practice make them so in law, or was the government, as the original, pre-18th century source of their authority, the legal holder of that title? Moreover, if strikes did not involve disorder, were they still within the ambit of the law as interpreted by the 1908 Committee? These are very important questions and a central concern of this book, for if the magistrates were the civil authorities in 1908 it can be argued that they are still the civil authority today. If that is the true position, then post-1945 governments will have been, and still are, acting *ultra vires* in mobilising troops in the majority of strikes.

The arguments for and against this interpretation will be developed later but it is important to note here that, in the very serious strikes of 1910-14 the use of troops by the government was widely thought to be unconstitutional or even illegal, and that the government itself did not produce a coherent case in its own support. What the government did say was that 'the military authorities always enjoy power to move troops in their own country'[21] (see next section for a full account of these events), and this is the essence of claims by governments today that they are exercising a royal prerogative power when they send troops into strikes. Before the First World War this fledgling idea was condemned, along with the rest of the government's actions, as 'treasonable' (see page 31). How this 'treason' may have become part of the law of this country is one of the subjects examined by the rest of this chapter.

The forces available for strike-breaking had been reorganised over the years before 1909. Governments had realised for decades that troops should only be used in strikes or riots as a last resort as their presence often caused more trouble than it quelled. The growth of the police from the mid-19th century had enabled the military to withdraw from public order and strike duties to a large degree as the unarmed police proved a more publicly acceptable instrument of control, although troops were called out to aid the civil power on 24 occasions between 1869 and 1908.[22]

Today's sophisticated and elaborate contingency planning apparatus for strike-breaking was virtually unknown in 1909. Governments, until the beginning of the 20th century, had a non-interventionist approach to the economy and industry and, therefore, to industrial disputes, and consequently there was no significant contingency planning carried out by the government department responsible, the Home Office. Strikes were dealt with pragmatically; when a serious strike occurred the government — if it knew anything about in advance — would usually wait until the magistrates (or, after Featherstone, the magistrates and/or the county police) informed them of the situation and asked for assistance. Improvements in police inter-force co-ordination and the post-Featherstone changes in the role of the magistrates by the government to decrease local influence over strike-breaking, had resulted in a smoother process for coping with strikes; but central direction and planning was effectively non-existent, except during the emergency itself.

1910-14: From Bending The Law To Breaking It

The near insurrection and major strikes of 1910-14 turned the Edwardian strike-controlling system on its head. The apparent law became such a barrier to effective strike-breaking that the government had to break the law openly. Rifle-shooting and bayonet-wielding troops turned the clock back 100 years to replace the overwhelmed police, and central planning and direction was seen to be an urgent necessity. The old system failed because the nature of the problems it was expected to solve was changing rapidly.

Between 1910 and 1914 working people were in a more rebellious mood than at any time since the 1840s, as real wages declined while prices and employers' profits were on the increase: 'The realisation of the workers that they were growing poorer just at the time when their employers were growing richer . . . accounts for the bitterness of the great strike struggles of the early years of the present century. No such open class antagonism had been seen in Britain since the time of the Chartists.'[23]

The new unions of the semi-skilled and unskilled workers had grown rapidly; between 1900 and 1914 trade union membership rose from 2,022,000 to 4,145,000.[24] Twenty-nine Labour MPs were elected in the 1906 general election, and a 'reforming' Liberal Government adopted new social and trade union legislation. But the working class's declining economic position was left untouched and, consequently, by 1910 many workers had become disillusioned and turned to industrial action, particularly that advocated by Syndicalism, as a way of improving their conditions.

The strikes that produced the first serious disorder were by coalminers in South Wales in 1910. The riots at Tonypandy in November of that year showed just how unsatisfactory the locally-controlled system for quelling disorder could be for governments trying to implement national economic and public order policies. Robin Evelegh explained what happened in his book *Peace-keeping in a Democratic Society*:

> 'These riots resulted from a strike in South Wales by miners against the colliery owners. The magistrates concerned were mostly appointed from among the directors or shareholders of the Cambrian Collieries Company, whose collieries were involved in the dispute. The local police tended to be employed as a strike-breaking force operated for the benefit of the coal-owners. Thus, the local civil authority and the local police were parties to the dispute causing the civil disturbances.'[25]

The Chief Constable of Glamorgan, finding himself unable to control the disturbances, asked the local army commander for troops without first consulting the Home Office. The Home Secretary, Winston Churchill, was furious. He immediately halted the military deployment and sent instead a force of Metropolitan Police officers to try to restore order, only mobilising troops when this measure failed. Churchill:

> 'was not prepared to put the military in support of the local magistrates or to leave the police under their control. Moreover, he did not wish to repeat the separation of control between the civil and military authorities that had caused problems on other similar occasions. Churchill therefore sent Major-General Nevil Macready from the War Office to act as the representative of central Government and to take command of both the police and the military in suppressing disorder. Thus the constitutional theory was turned upside down.'[26]

August 1911 saw the old public order/strike-breaking procedure near to collapse when many disputes fused together in what almost became the first modern general strike. Churchill called it: '. . . a new force in trade unionism. . . The general strike is a factor that must be dealt with.'[27]

In that one month, four people were shot dead by the army and soldiers made numerous bayonet charges on crowds in the riots that accompanied the strikes or the presence of the military. Nearly all the regular troops in Britain were mobilised or put on standby to suppress these civil disorders.

The serious disturbances had begun in Cardiff in late July 1911 when workers in many industries joined seamen striking for union recognition. Troops were sent in after a dock warehouse was burned down. By the beginning of August, a major dock strike had also started on the Thames and there were signs of a dispute coming on the railways. The Port of London was paralysed by the end of the first week of August and, when soldiers unloaded a ship in the docks, the strikers warned that a breach of the peace would follow if they did not stop. By 10 August the situation was critical, with 80,000 on strike, serious violence taking place on the streets and food stocks beginning to run low.

Churchill wanted to confront the strikers and over 20,000 troops at Aldershot, Woolwich and Shorncliffe were issued with ammunition and rations and made ready to move into London. The Prime Minister, Herbert Asquith, and other senior ministers were against the use of troops but before any deployments were made the employers conceded to the strikers' demands on 11 August.

The day before the dock strike ended, however, 400 soldiers of the 2nd Worcestershire Regiment were ordered to Liverpool where a strike amongst transport and associated workers was about to start. A lock-out of the city's 25,000 dockers on 14 August sparked off severe rioting and, that night, troops fired shots over the heads of one crowd and bayonet-charged another.

The following day, five prison vans carrying convicted rioters of the night before to the city's Walton Gaol were intercepted by a 3,000-strong angry crowd in Vauxhall Road. A cavalry escort of Hussars and Scots Greys opened fire, killing two people. The van drivers and cavalry then fought their way through the crowd to the gaol where infantry soldiers and mounted police joined in a pitched battle that lasted nearly an hour. More bayonet charges were made over the next few days and, on 17 August, a Royal Navy cruiser, HMS *Antrim,* sailed into the Mersey in an attempt to overawe the population. A second cruiser arrived soon after.

The most serious disorder of the year came, however, when Britain's first national rail strike started on 18 August. Two hundred thousand rail workers struck immediately and rioting quickly broke out in many areas of the country. Thirteen thousand armed soldiers were at once sent into central London, setting up camp in the main parks, the Tower of London and the General Post Office while numerous incidents of military operations with loaded rifles and fixed bayonets against strikers were reported.

The most bloody event occurred at Llanelli on 19 August, when strikers stopped a train carrying blackleg workers. Soldiers of the Worcestershire Regiment then advanced on the strikers with fixed bayonets but the crowd stood its ground and some even laughed when the Riot Act was read. The strikers refused to believe that warning shots fired over their heads were real and instead moved towards the soldiers. The troops could then only flee or shoot: they opened fire, killing two strikers and injuring several others. The same evening, angry crowds attacked the home of a magistrate who had been involved in reading the Riot Act and looted his shop in the town. When they later set fire to a railway store, there was an explosion and four more people were killed.

The rail strike lasted only a few more days but the civil unrest continued for some time afterwards. At its height 58,000 troops were deployed in 35 towns and cities, mainly in Yorkshire, Lancashire, the Midlands and Wales.

In this dire emergency, the government resorted to the extensive use of military force, although this meant ignoring the constitution and the law.

As Churchill said: 'I do not know whether in the history of the world a similar catastrophe can be shown to have menaced an equally great community.'[29] He described the situation thus: 'The conditions which have undoubtedly occurred in the last week have been without any previous experience in this country.'[30]

Instead of waiting for magistrates in the localities to requisition troops the government imposed what its critics called a form of martial law by handing over strike-breaking responsibility to a hastily formed joint organisation of the War Office and the Home Office, dominated by the military. The chief centres of disturbances were divided into seven Strike Areas, each run by a senior officer reporting direct to the War Office. The Strike Area Commanders had full control over the troops under them: there was no question of the civil authorities, constitutionally responsible for maintaining order, exercising any influence. Troops were deployed around the towns and countryside *whether or not* their presence had been requested.

Churchill explained the government's extreme actions, first, by arguing they had to do something: 'No government could possibly sit still with folded hands and say: "A trade dispute is going on. We must remain impartial".'[31] Just what the government could do was the subject of some confusion, however, even to Churchill. On 17 August, the day before the railway strike started, he said: 'There can be no question of the military forces of the Crown intervening in a labour dispute. . . . It is only when a trade dispute is accompanied by riot, intimidation or other violations of the law or when a serious interruption is caused or likely to be caused to the supply of necessary commodities, that the military can be called on to support the police; and then their duty is to maintain the law, not to interfere in the matter in dispute.'[32]

After five days of the rail strike, however, Churchill saw the law rather differently: 'The military authorities always enjoy power to move troops in their own country — to move British troops about the country wherever it is found to be convenient or necessary, and the regulation which has hitherto restricted their employment in places where there was disorder until there had been a requisition from the local authority was only a regulation for the convenience of the War Office and generally of the government, and has in these circumstances necessarily been abrogated in order to enable the military authorities to discharge the duties with which at this juncture they were officially charged.'[33]

In other words, Churchill was saying that the common law position on the use of troops in disturbances, enshrined in the Army Regulations since 1769, was not the law but merely an internal guideline for the military which could be changed at will.

The government's illegal actions were widely condemned by MPs, trade unionists and members of the public. A labour movement meeting in Trafalgar Square on 26 August called the government's behaviour 'treasonable suppression of civil authority' and the 'institution of martial law'. George Lansbury moved the principal motion at the meeting condemning 'the unconstitutional doctrine laid down and enforced by the Home Secretary with the approval of his colleagues by which the various military districts were given a free hand in the disposal and use of the troops under their command, independent of and in opposition to the civil authorities.'[34] In the House of Commons Keir Hardie said: 'Talk about revolution! The law of England has been broken in the interests of the railway companies.'[35] The men shot down at Llanelli, Hardie went on had been 'murdered by the Government in the interests of the capitalist system.'[36]

The significance of 1911 is that it was the watershed between the old and the new approach to military strike-breaking. It showed, first, that using the old methods, the government could not handle even a limited national rail strike without the army having to shoot down people on the streets. But the strikers also learned that all-out strikes in vital industries like the docks and the railways were eminently winnable. In an increasingly interdependent society the government was going to have to work out a way of breaking these strikes without resorting to a level of violence that was counterproductive.

The only realisable solution to this problem was for the government to mobilise an alternative labour force to replace the strikers peacefully — and to give itself the legal power to do so. Nine years later the government was to take this momentous step when it enacted the Emergency Powers Act 1920.

Despite the many and bitter protests against the Asquith government's unconstitutional activities in the 1911 strikes, surprisingly, its actions were not challenged in the courts.

Churchill's responses to the accusation that his government had acted illegally are very relevant today, however, as they were the first attempts by a government, first to deny that the common law circumscribed the government's ability to mobilise troops for strike-breaking and, secondly, to lay claim instead to some other power to deploy troops at will in strikes.

Nevertheless, little was to be heard of this argument until troops first began to be used on a large scale as blacklegs (rather than as a substitute police force) in the late 1940s. As we shall see in the next section, if this power really existed, then the very time it was needed most, perhaps, was immediately after the end of the First World War. Instead of claiming such a right however, the Coalition government of 1920 seemed convinced that the only way it could use troops legally as blacklegs was by passing a special Act of Parliament.

Unlawful Orders and Emergency Powers

The First World War defused what was widely thought to be a potential revolution in Britain. The outbreak of the war led to the passing of the Defence of the Realm Act (or DORA as it was less than affectionately known) which gave the government wide powers to direct civil life, including some control over strikes; but the external enemy, Germany, preoccupied the government until 1918.

At the end of the war, however, the threat of a union-led uprising reappeared with the trade union movement in a stronger position and an even more aggressive mood than in 1914. The successful 1917 Russian revolution had also helped inspire the British working class into unprecedented action, such as the soldiers and police strikes of 1919. The 1919 Liverpool police strike was the last occasion on which a person was shot dead by soldiers on public order duties in Britain until the Iranian Embassy siege of 1980.

Within a few months of the war ending, the government's attention was very firmly focused on the problems of maintaining internal security and public order. In their book *States of*

Emergency Keith Jeffery and Peter Hennessy write:

> 'The possibility of revolution in Britain following the First
> World War lay not so much in the likelihood of armed
> insurrection or a workers' coup of some sort, but in the more
> subtle, and to some more insidious, challenge posed to the state
> by an extra-governmental power centre — the trade unions. The
> unprecedented strength of trade unionism after the war revived
> pre-war syndicalist ideas, and in particular the notion of
> concerted nation-wide action in a general strike. Since the
> development of wartime collectivism had to a very great extent
> placed the government, rather than the owners, in control of
> industry, labour ambitions readily resolved into direct
> confrontation between unions and government. In these
> circumstances the line between industrial and political power
> was fine indeed. It seems that the labour movement might
> acquire extensive political power, not in the formal electoral
> sense, but from simple *force majeure*. Problems were posed,
> therefore, concerning the ultimate legitimacy of the state to
> rule.'[37]

Jeffrey and Hennessy conclude: 'It is questionable, however,
whether the post-war industrial unrest was in any real sense
"revolutionary",'[38] but that nonetheless 'an underlying fear of
revolution sharpened the official response to strikes'.[39]

This response took two forms; first, a rapid development and
activation of the contingency planning apparatus which emerged in
the First World War, including involvement of the military (see
page 39 below); and second, an important change in the law
relating to military intervention in strikes.

The law was problematic because, for nearly two years after the
war ended, the government relied on the wartime Defence of the
Realm Act for the legal powers it needed to suppress industrial
unrest — but it was by no means certain that DORA did actually
apply in peacetime. No formal challenge was made to the legality of
the government's use of DORA, however, but officials nonetheless
were sensitive to the delicacy of the path they were treading in
suppressing serious industrial disturbances by a possibly illegal
means.

The problem was highlighted in early 1920 when it became
known that troops could lawfully refuse to replace striking workers
because it was not strictly a military duty.

This question of the lawfulness of orders given to troops was —
and still is — a central concern of senior military officers and
politicians for, if troops could refuse to obey commands, then the

foundations of the state's last line of defence against insurrection would disintegrate. Labour MPs had shown interest in this topic in 1912 when they claimed that troops were no more obliged to obey blacklegging orders than were civilians.[40] This arose during the course of the annual debate on the renewal of the Army (Annual) Act, when Labour unsuccessfully proposed an amendment allowing new recruits to opt out of strike-breaking duties. The amendment was put forward because of the events of 1911 and similar amendments, providing a rare opportunity for MPs to criticise the internal use of the military, were tabled on at least eight subsequent occasions during the annual debates on the renewal of the Act until 1934.

In the looming industrial chaos of 1919 and 1920, the government decided it had to clarify whether these 'blacklegging' orders to troops were legal. It was told that they were not. The Judge Advocate-General, Sir Felix Cassel, was asked whether or not troops could legally be given orders to replace striking workers and whether orders so given were lawful commands rendering troops who disobeyed them liable to the proceedings laid down in the military discipline acts. He replied, in a secret communication in January 1920: 'I am of the opinion that a soldier cannot lawfully be commanded to perform vital services except under the following conditions: (a) if and insofar as some military object, purpose or proceeding . . . is affected, or (b) if such a condition of affairs has arisen that the safety of the realm and the existence of the King's Government and authority are endangered and His Majesty, acting through his responsible Ministers to save the State, has decided to entrust any such service or services to military administration and control.'[41] He clarified what he meant in point (a) by saying that: 'A soldier can be required to run trains conveying troops or military stores or munitions, but not trains carrying civilian passengers or traffic'.[42] The Law Officers of the Crown later said they agreed with the Judge Advocate's opinion.[43]

The political implications of these findings, if they had become public, would have been explosive. In the highly charged climate of the time, the revelation that the government could not legally order troops to break strikes could simultaneously have destroyed the credibility of the government and spurred working class leaders to new heights of militancy. The findings were, therefore, kept secret.

The government was clearly going to have to do something very quickly to legalise blacklegging orders, and this highlighted the need to pass a law replacing DORA, then expected to 'expire' in the autumn of 1920. Widespread industrial unrest was expected late in 1920 and the government, early in the year, drafted a law that would go beyond even DORA's provisions by expressly allowing the government to use troops as blacklegs. This preparation was carried out in great secrecy because, as the government admitted to itself: 'The Bill is of a drastic character, the object is to give the government full powers to meet a potentially revolutionary situation.'[44]

This Bill, which was to become the Emergency Powers Act 1920, was drafted in such general terms that it solved the same problem of legalising the orders given to troops without making it obvious that the problem had ever existed. But the Emergency Powers Act 1920 only covered the most serious strikes that could be called emergencies under the Act. As we shall see, when troops were required for less than 'revolutionary situations' from 1945 onwards, other laws had to be passed to legalise the orders given to troops.

It should be noted here that the government in 1920 seemed convinced that the only way it could legally mobilise troops for blacklegging was by passing a special Act of Parliament, in complete contrast to the claims of governments today that they do not need statutory authority, as strike-breaking is covered by the Royal Prerogative. Lloyd George's government, in enacting the Emergency Powers Act, was implicitly agreeing with the traditional common law position that legal strike-breaking in the absence of the emergency law, could only be initiated by the magistrates.

The public did not know (because of official secrecy) that Lloyd George's government had apparently conceded that governments could not legally break strikes where no state of emergency was declared. Consequently, trade unionists were unaware that subsequent governments could not, lawfully, adopt this halfway position between not intervening militarily in a strike and declaring a state of emergency. The decrease in industrial activity after the collapse of the General Strike until the Second World War temporarily buried the issue because troops were not needed for strike-breaking during that period.

The Emergency Powers Act 1920

After much discussion, Lloyd George's government decided to keep its Emergency Powers Bill firmly under wraps until the last possible moment, as 'the introduction of a measure of this sort would certainly raise highly contentious questions and might precipitate the crisis which it is desired to avoid.'[45] The Bill was unveiled in October 1920, when with the end of the short-lived post-war economic boom, the coalminers came out on strike and their allies in the Triple Alliance, the railway and transport unions, threatened to take supportive action that could have brought the country to a standstill.[46] The government bought itself a breathing space of a few months by giving the miners a temporary wage rise, while using this opportunity to rush through parliament its Emergency Powers Act 1920 which remains the main piece of strike-breaking legislation. The Act enables governments to use any means necessary, including deploying troops, to deal with certain types of national emergencies, particularly strikes. Despite its wide scope, the Act was specifically designed, and has only been used, for breaking strikes.[47]

The Labour MP Sidney Silverman recalled, during the parliamentary debate on the later Emergency Powers Act 1964 his memories of how the 1920 Act was passed:

'The 1920 Government was elected on a war-time coupon — the then Mr Lloyd George's coupon election — in a wave of triumph, as a vote of thanks from the country. It was a parliament consisting of what the late Professor J.M. Keynes described as a lot of hard-faced men who looked as if they had done very well out of the war. But it was not only that; they set themselves to do very well out of the peace, too. All kinds of controls were removed. Millions of men were simultaneously let loose on the labour market, in a country which had not even begun to adapt itself to the change-over from war-time to peace-time conditions. Indeed, for years after that it would have been a very optimistic Member of the House of Commons who could have described the period as peace-time.

In those circumstances . . . there was a serious danger of industrial disruption and, perhaps, subversion. To guard themselves against the anger of the people, arising out of the chaos that the post-war government had produced, that government felt bound to arm themselves with these extreme powers, and they found no difficulty in getting through their measure in a parliament constituted as it then was. Nevertheless, outside the House, the measure was fiercely resisted. It did not go through in a calm and peaceful atmosphere . . . There were meetings throughout the country. There were gatherings that amounted almost to riotous assemblies, because people did not like to see any government — and least of all that government — arming themselves with such supreme powers as that Act provided, in suitable circumstances.'[48]

The Emergency Powers Act 1920 at last cleared a track through the legal constraints on, and confusion over, the use of troops against the civilian population — but only in 'emergencies'.

Only by declaring a state of emergency under the Act can a government give itself temporary powers to use troops to break major strikes in many (but not all) key industries.

The Act in no way removed or resolved the basic legal and constitutional constraints on and uncertainties over military blacklegging in 'normal' times. At the end of a state of emergency, the government was still not the civil authority empowered to call out the troops, soldiers could still lawfully disobey strike-breaking orders and the question of just how much force could be used remained unanswered. The Act simply enabled the government to overcome these constraints temporarily by suspending these and other aspects of the constitution and by giving the needs of the state priority over the historic rights of its citizens.

The Emergency Powers Act served its purpose in the 1920s by helping the state to survive a near revolution. But after World War Two it was to prove to be far too big a sledgehammer for the smaller nuts that then needed cracking, with its dramatic proclamations of a state of emergency by the monarch, repeated debates in parliament and the accompanying, heightened public tension. As Bonar Law, Leader of the House of Commons, said on introducing the measure into parliament in 1920: 'This Bill is not intended to apply, and could not by any possibility apply, to any ordinary industrial dispute between employers and workmen.'[49] From 1945 another method of legalising blacklegging would be necessary.

Twelve states of emergency have been declared under the Emergency Powers Act 1920, all of them to handle industrial disputes. Nine of these have been declared since 1945, five of them between 1970 and 1974. Troops intervened in eight of these 12 disputes: the 1921 miners strike, 1926 General Strike, 1948 and 1949 dock strikes, 1955 railway strike, 1966 seamens strike, 1970 power workers overtime ban and the 1972 dock strikes. The four other emergencies, when there was no military intervention, were during the 1924 London tram drivers strike, 1970 dock strike, 1972 miners strike and the 1973-74 miners strike and energy crisis. States of emergency have usually been declared where the government needs to take action which would otherwise be illegal, for example requisitioning private vehicles or suspending power supplies. Where such drastic action is not necessary, governments, particularly since 1974, have invoked other procedures (see chapter two).

The Act says: 'If at any time it appears to His Majesty that any action has been taken or is immediately threatened by any persons or body of persons of such a nature and on so extensive a scale as to be calculated, by interfering with the supply and distribution of food, water, fuel or light, or with the means of locomotion, to deprive the community, or any substantial portion of the community, of the essentials of life, His Majesty may, by proclamation, . . . declare that a state of emergency exists.'

It should be emphasised here that it is not parliament that decides whether an emergency exists, it is the cabinet, which then gives its action constitutional and public legitimacy by using the monarchy to make the proclamation.

The proclamation has to be 'communicated to Parliament' within five days and it has to be renewed after one month. Once the proclamation has been made, regulations for 'securing the essentials of life to the community' can be introduced. These give the government 'such powers and duties as His Majesty may deem necessary for the preservation of the peace, for securing and regulating the supply and distribution of food, water, fuel, light and other necessities, for maintaining the means of transit or locomotion, and for any other purposes essential to the public safety and the life of the community.'[51]

Once a state of emergency has been declared any government can give itself virtually unlimited power by using the Act. The only constraints specified in law are that there can be no form of 'compulsory military service or industrial conscription', striking and picketing are to remain legal and existing criminal procedure cannot be altered. The original Bill did not even contain these safeguards, while the government before publishing the Bill, had also wanted to extend it to Ireland.[52]

There seems to be little scope for challenging powers taken under the Act in British courts but Gillian Morris in her detailed analysis believes that the law may fall outside the European Convention on Human Rights through its over generous definition of what constitutes an emergency.[53]

Morris also says: '. . . while the Emergency Powers Act appears to guarantee parliamentary control over the exercise of its powers (when these powers are taken for any length of time) in practice the extent of this control is limited and compliance with the procedure is more a matter of form than an effective method of restraining the excesses of the executive.'[54] The proclamation of an emergency only has to be 'communicated' to parliament, not approved by it, and any regulations made are only submitted for parliamentary approval *after* they have been put into effect.

The major factor that limits the use of the 1920 Act is that a state of emergency can only be proclaimed where the 'essentials of life' for at least a substantial portion of the community are threatened by people 'interfering with the supply and distribution of food, water, fuel or light, or with the means of locomotion.' (S.1(1); the later Emergency Powers Act 1964 extended the 1920 Act to cover threats from any source, not just people (see pp.52-3 below).)

The Act was used in its intended manner to save the government from possible defeat in the serious 1926 General Strike, but it is questionable if the other occasion on which it was activated between the two World Wars — by the first Labour government during the 1924 London tram drivers strike — in fact met the Act's criteria of depriving a 'substantial portion' of the community of the essentials of life. The same doubts can be raised over the other non-national emergencies, in the London docks in 1948 and 1949. These two emergencies saw the introduction of 'damage to the economy' as a partial justification for declaring the emergency, a criterion clearly not in the 1920 Act, but this was to be the main reasoning for declaring the 1966 emergency.

A further legal problem with the Emergency Powers Act 1920 has been pointed out by Jeffery and Hennessy in their book *States of Emergency*. They describe how: 'during the preparation of a draft code of regulations, Parliamentary Counsel had raised doubts, later confirmed by the Law Officers, as to the legality of certain regulations previously made under the Emergency Powers Act relating to administrative duties performed by local authorities. Section 2(1) of the Act conferred powers on the government "or any other persons in His Majesty's service or acting on His Majesty's behalf." The Law Officers declared that this provision was "not sufficiently wide to include a statutory local authority", whose employees are not civil servants.'[55] In the 1926 General Strike parts of the Supply and Transport Organisation, the government's emergency planning body, had therefore operated illegally by depending on local authorities for food and coal distribution schemes.

When this problem was discovered by the Law Officers in March 1936 the Cabinet committee responsible for emergencies, the Supply and Transport Committee, discussed whether it should carry on as before, amend the Emergency Powers Act or bring in 'entirely new machinery'. The latter two alternatives were dismissed as potentially too provocative and the first course was therefore adopted. But the committee 'also agreed that a draft Bill amending the Emergency Powers Act could be prepared "for introduction at a suitable opportunity". Such an opportunity never arose and section 2(1) of the Act remains unamended.'[56]

The Machinery of Contingency Planning

The years immediately after the First World War saw not only the arming of the state with the legal power to break certain major strikes through the Emergency Powers Act 1920, but also the setting up of the contingency planning machinery that was necessary both to identify and to plan against the increasing number of potentially disruptive disputes.

In the apparently near-revolutionary days of 1919-20 the problems with the law were almost eclipsed by the possible threats to the actual existence of the British state. The military, reluctantly it appears, played a central role in the maintenance of public order as the police staggered under the weight of the demands on them, with troops, armoured vehicles and warships being deployed around the country at various times in response to potential or actual strikes.

The strikes that posed the biggest threat to the state were national ones, with a general strike of several unions acting together being the greatest fear. The pre-war local *ad hoc* strike-breaking arrangements were now inadequate and a centrally co-ordinated national response was needed. To achieve this, the Lloyd George coalition government, drawing on its administrative experiences in the war, rapidly experimented with and set up a centralised strike-breaking machinery that remains essentially the same today.

Government contingency planning began in early 1919, very soon after the war ended. On 4 February 1919, the Cabinet set up a sub-committee, the Industrial Unrest Committee, to make plans for industrial emergencies. A few days later the pre-war triple alliance of miners, transport and railways unions was re-formed and the army Commander-in-Chief for Great Britain was told to prepare his troops for a possible national strike. A military circular was sent round to local army commanders asking how reliable they thought their troops would be if called on to act in a strike. The results were not encouraging for the government; as Churchill said: 'All the reports deprecate the employment of troops in strike-breaking, and it would not be fair to ask troops to do what they consider to be blackleg work.'[57]

This issue became a particularly sensitive one for the government as the 'secret' circular was printed by the labour movement newspaper, the *Daily Herald*.[58] As a result of the ensuing public protests, the TUC annual conference unanimously condemned the government's action, one speaker saying: 'We are not going to allow our members to join the army in order to be turned into blacklegs and strike-breakers under government compulsion.'[59]

Industrial unrest increased during the second half of 1919, with a miners strike in Yorkshire in July requiring the intervention of 900 naval ratings, police strikes in August, including that in Liverpool where one man was shot dead by the army, and the railway strike in September which the government feared would become a general strike through the involvement of the triple alliance.

The Industrial Unrest Committee was accordingly disbanded in September and replaced by the much tougher Strike Committee, chaired by Sir Eric Geddes. The strike started on 26 September and, the following day, the mobilisation of 23,000 troops began with the aim of securing key points and installations. The strike ended one week later, however, with a settlement broadly favourable to the railway workers, just as the government was trying to establish some sort of 'third force' as an intermediate stage between the police and military.

On 14 October a new Cabinet committee, the Supply and Transport Committee (STC) replaced the Strike Committee with the task of continuing emergency planning and ensuring that the lessons of the railway strike were not lost. Geddes was again in the chair. In November the Cabinet agreed that a small contingency planning organisation should be maintained for future emergencies.

The military had some very pointed statements to make about what they had learned from the strike. Sir Douglas Haig, Commander-in-Chief Great Britain, observed that the army should not have had to take over from the police their duty of maintaining the King's peace. Sir George Macdonogh, Adjutant-General and responsible for the army's internal security plans, said: 'It seems to me that we have been attempting to perform duties which appertain to the civil power, and that in so doing we have not merely greatly strained the military machine but the British Constitution as well. We should insist on the Home Office doing its own work, i.e. preserving public order. It is only when the civil power has been proved powerless to carry out this work that the military should be called in. . . . It will be a bad day for the Empire if the Government of this country had to look to the bayonets of its troops for its support.'[60]

The post-war contingency planning system relied a great deal initially on the military and their resources, but the rapid run-down of the services after 1919, plus the military's professed reluctance to be involved in internal security duties in Britain, helped spur on the development of civilian capabilities.

The army made it clear after the 1919 railway strike that it would be unlikely to be able to help the police on the same scale in future because of the cutbacks in personnel.

The first few months of 1920 saw revolution still threatening and the army still having to provide major support to the police. When a miners strike appeared likely in March, 11 regional Commissioners were appointed for England and Wales, the forerunner of today's regional contingency planning system.

By this time, the emergencies organisation, 'which had developed largely on an *ad hoc* basis to meet the strikes of 1919, was established on a systematic footing. It was to underpin the government's policy towards major strikes for the next 20 years.'[61]

The first major test of the plans came when the miners decided to strike on 16 October 1920. By 22 October, troops, tanks and armoured cars were being despatched around the country, and a battleship was sent to Liverpool. That same day, the Home Secretary brought the Emergency Powers Bill before the House of Commons (see above). A threat by the railway workers to intervene led to the government giving the miners a temporary pay rise within a few days, but the Bill was still pushed through parliament because it was going to be needed in future.

The miners dispute resurfaced on 31 March 1921, when the wartime nationalisation of the mines was ended and the government handed them back to their former owners. The next day, 1 April, the owners locked out the miners and a state of emergency was declared by the government. A strike by the triple alliance now looked probable and all sides made preparations, with the government again deploying troops, armoured cars and tanks. The other members of the triple alliance were expected to join the miners on strike on Friday 15 April and the Supply and Transport Organisation (STO) was fully activated the day before in readiness for it. But on the day itself, 'Black Friday', divisions within the union ranks led to the railway and transport workers deciding not to strike and the miners were eventually defeated.

The emergencies organisation was steadily run down from the summer of 1921 as industrial militancy declined. In 1923, however, Baldwin's Conservative government (elected in October 1922) authorised a review of contingency planning by Sir John Anderson, Permanent Under Secretary at the Home Office and, as head of the emergency organisation from 1922-32, one of the key figures in the early years of emergency planning. His report, on 5 July 1923, recommended that the government should have emergency plans available, with an *ad hoc* Cabinet committee.[62] Less than a week later, the Supply and Transport Committee was re-established in response to unofficial dock strikes and Anderson's report was used as the model for the organisation. The dock strikes came to nothing but led the Cabinet to agree to the full implementation of Anderson's proposals and the remainder of 1923 saw a re-examination of the emergency plans of 1919-21.

Britain's first Labour government took office on 22 January 1924, without a working majority. Ideologically opposed to government strike-breaking, the Labour government inherited from the Conservatives a strike by railway workers for which the

Supply and Transport Organisation had been activated on 20 January and the Cabinet had little choice but to continue its mobilisation. A dock strike in February 1924 forced Ramsay MacDonald's Cabinet to consider contingency planning in detail and ministers decided that they too should use Anderson's report, although largely unsuccessful attempts were made to end some of the secrecy surrounding the planing and to involve trade unionists in it.

The Labour government's worst trial came with the March 1924 strike by London tram and bus drivers, when a state of emergency was declared, possibly without sufficient justification under the terms laid down in the Emergency Powers Act 1920. The proclamation of the emergency was revoked after only one day, however, and the powers were not used as the employers made the drivers an acceptable wage offer. The Cabinet was reluctant to activate the STO for the strike but 'there is no evidence to suggest that they did not intend to use it if really necessary.'[63]

Labour only held on to power until November 1924, when the Conservatives returned with a healthy majority, under the leadership once more of Stanley Baldwin. They took up contingency planning where they had dropped it at the beginning of the year and, within four weeks of resuming control, had appointed a new STC and re-established the STO.

The War Office had not stopped making plans while the Labour Government was in office, however, and had a memorandum on how it saw its duties in aid of the civil power circulating within a few days of Baldwin taking over again. This memorandum was to provide the basis for the military plan operated during the 1926 General Strike.

This review of contingency planning was spurred on to a conclusion by a serious dispute in the coal industry in July 1925. This ended on 31 July ('Red Friday') in what was widely seen as a victory for the miners. The government gave a subsidy of £23 million to boost miners pay packets for nine months and the owners backed away from a confrontation to support the government's proposal for a major commission of inquiry into the coal industry, chaired by Sir Herbert Samuel.

It later became clear that this was only a temporary retreat by the government and mine owners, biding their time while emergency machinery was fully tuned up and public sympathy for the miners was given a chance to decline. When Samuel's report was rejected by the mine owners and the wage subsidy ran out in April 1926, the miners prepared to go on strike, backed by the other members of the triple alliance. But by then the government's strike-breaking machine was ready for them.

The General Strike of May 1926 is a unique, momentous event in British history. More than two million workers came out on strike in a bitter, but largely bloodless, revolt. Both sides accused the other of having declared some sort of war, Baldwin stating that union leaders were 'going nearer to proclaiming civil war than we have been for centuries past.'[64]

The immediate cause of the strike was the mine owners' announcement that they were going to cut miners' wages from 1 May. The strike began at midnight on 3 May and ended just nine days later with the strikers defeated. The remaining years before the Second World War saw the Labour movement on the defensive and unable to resist the effects of the recession of the 1930s. The strike came so near to success, however, that it frightened both the government and trade union leaders away from policies of confrontation to those of industrial *detente* and no major strike since has come so close to challenging the fundamental structure of British society.

The Baldwin government's success in the strike was due at least in part to its ability to preserve an orderly system of government and maintain some essential services and supplies. The way the government could do this was proposed in a STC memorandum of 6 August 1925 which described the detailed plans then ready, or being prepared for the looming strike.[65] A Royal Commission which preceded the strike failed to avert it but gave the government ample time to finalise and implement these plans.

The STC memo showed that under the STC was a standing sub-committee which, in an emergency, would split into separate, essential service committees handling communications, finance, food, fuel, 'protection' (mainly public order), publicity and transport. In command would be the Chief Civil Commissioner, with 11 Civil Commissioners (ministers) below him administering the nine divisions of England, plus Scotland and Wales. Below the divisions, the country had been further split into 88 areas, in each of which there was a Volunteer Service Committee composed of local representatives of the national essential service committees. The VSCs were to recruit volunteers for strike-hit national services (transport, mail, docks etc), while key local utilities (gas, water etc) were the responsibility of the local authorities. The national essential services committees also had their own regional structures which made the necessary detailed plans and liaised with each other through the divisional organisation.

The plans outlined in the August memo 'were based upon the principle of using normal commercial channels to distribute supplies. Whereas during the 1919 railway strike the government had assumed direct control of the supply and distribution of food and essential commodities, the aim in 1925 was to throw the responsibility on to committees manned very largely by the main businessmen in each trade. By the end of the First World War there were trade associations in nearly all industries and it was to these organisations that the government had turned in preparing its plans.'[66]

The STC memo also gave the police the primary responsibility for the maintenance of law and order; the army were only to be called on in an emergency. Police numbers were to be boosted by the recruitment of 100,000 special constables.

After the Cabinet had discussed the STC memo, secret steps were taken to begin implementing it. By October 1925, offices had been established for all 11 divisions and 82 of the areas, and four-fifths of the officers had been appointed. There had been no government action to recruit volunteers but, on 25 September, the unofficial Organisation for the Maintenance of Supplies had been set up under Lord Hardinge of Penshurst to begin enlisting potential strike-breakers and the government did not try seriously to distance itself from the new body.

In late November, the government relaxed secrecy and issued a circular to local authorities telling them of its plans for the possible strike and asking for their co-operation. They were to be put into operation on the receipt of a telegram from the government saying simply 'Action'. 'Every eventuality appears to have been covered by this time and the government was as well prepared as if it had been facing a threat of civil insurrection.'[67] The more belligerent members of the Cabinet (including Churchill) 'waited eagerly for May to come.'[68]

The General Strike began late on Monday 3 May and was called off by the TUC on the 12th. The government declared a state of emergency three days before the strike started and kept it in existence until 19 December, as the miners did not finally go back to work until late November. The government's strike-breaking plan was immediately activated and worked smoothly and efficiently throughout the strike.

The military were kept in the background as far as possible during the strike, although they were used to a limited extent both to assist the police in keeping order and to replace some strikers.

The military were mobilised in a public order role to escort food convoys, notably through the pickets of the London docks, to protect power stations and other key installations and to cordon off the Whitehall area. In addition, army units were moved to camps in or near all large cities, while Royal Navy ships sailed into all main ports.[69] RAF fighters piloted by reservists and armed with live ammunition were reported to have patrolled railway lines.[70]

The strike-breaking role of troops was even more limited, their main uses being to replace some strikers in the London docks and in 33 London power stations.[71] Submarines were brought into London's Royal Docks to provide electricity from their batteries for meat cold stores.

In contrast to the military's central role in all levels of the near-general strike of 1911, the armed forces in 1926 were largely kept in reserve as the new civil emergency government system co-ordinated both the keeping of order and strike breaking by police and volunteers. Nevertheless, 26 battalions, over a quarter of the army's total strength, were called out on emergency duty during the strike.[72]

Volunteers were prominent in the General Strike, but their usefulness to the government is questionable. The unofficial Organisation for the Maintenance of Supplies was conspicuous for the number of recruits it produced, but most of these were of the wrong type and/or in the wrong place.

The War Office successfully resisted moves to have the Territorial Army called up or to have a paramilitary third force created. The military's post-First World War experiences had convinced it that the primary duty for maintaining internal security should rest with the police and that any special forces that were raised should be attached to the police, not the military. Towards the end of the strike, on 10 May, a Civil Constabulary Reserve was set up to reinforce the police with civilian volunteers. This was an unarmed body under the control of the police but with recruiting and equipping carried out by the army, an apparently satisfactory arrangement for the War Office.[73]

The Police and the Military after the General Strike

From 1926 until 1939 there appears to have been no military involvement in strikes, either in public order or strike-breaking roles. This was primarily due to the absence of strikes threatening essential services and supplies. The reasons for this decline in industrial action compared with the pre-1926 period are numerous but prominent amongst them are the demoralising effects on the labour movement of both the recession of the late 1920s and 1930s and the defeat in the General Strike, plus the passing of the Labour Disputes and Trade Union Act 1927 which made sympathy strikes and mass picketing illegal (this was repealed by the Labour government in 1946). This relative peace was fortuitous for the governments of the late 1920s and 1930s as there was some doubt about the reduced post-war army's ability to handle a major internal crisis: 'The Chief of the Imperial General Staff's nightmare was Communist-inspired subversion at home coinciding with a major crisis overseas.'[74] The government's contingency planning system was not therefore, called on so much during this period and no further changes in the law of strike-breaking had to be attempted.

One issue that was finally settled (in theory at least) was that of the relationship between the military and the police in public order and strike-breaking duties. For nearly 100 years governments had been trying to withdraw the military from frequent armed interventions in civilian life in a law and order role and attempted, instead, to hand this responsibility over to the more publicly acceptable police. The military could then be kept in reserve for the most dire emergencies only, when exceptional firepower was needed. This process of giving primacy to the police suffered a serious setback in 1918 and 1919, however, when government confidence was shaken by the police strikes.

In the years immediately following this period, various combinations of the military and 'third forces' were experimented with until the loyalty of the police during the General Strike finally confirmed them in the role of civilian peacekeepers.

The General Strike was the last occasion when troops intervened in a strike in Britain to keep the peace and therefore marks a watershed in civil/military history, although this by no means rules out its future use in this role. Before 1926, troops had primarily been called on in strikes to display or inflict force that the police either did not possess or could not be relied on to deploy effectively. Since 1926, however, the police have been responsible for public order and troops have only intervened in strikes to replace the strikers or ameliorate the effects of their actions.

In the broader public order field, the police have coped unaided with civil disturbances since the General Strike (except in Northern Ireland) and the military have mainly acted in a MACP role for 'anti-terrorist' duties: for example Heathrow and Stansted Airports, providing bomb-disposal teams, storming the Iranian Embassy in 1980 and providing covert SAS-type squads for unspecified special duties.

Since 1926 it has therefore been possible to separate out military duties aimed at keeping order and those for strike-breaking, terms that were almost synonymous before the General Strike. The military themselves now talk of two separate military roles: Military Aid to the Civil Power (MACP) — aiding the police — and Military Aid to the Civil Ministries (MACM) — strike-breaking.

These now widely used terms are both misnomers that, intentionally or otherwise, conveniently help the public see the processes from the point of view of the government's practice rather than the legal theory which is partly opposed to it. For example, the police are not the 'civil power' as that role still belongs to the magistrates, while the 'civil ministries' (government departments) are not clearly legally empowered to call on troops in all strikes, a duty that may still rest with the magistrates in the majority of cases.*

*Although we are primarily concerned here with the role of troops in strikes it should be noted that the police also pay a part in industrial disputes, not only through enforcing the laws on picketing and public order, for example, but now also as blacklegs. During the ambulance crews dispute of early 1979 (see pages 143-4 below), when strikers refused to provide emergency cover, police took over their duties in what is believed to be 'the first occasion on which the police have undertaken jobs normally performed by strikers during an industrial dispute, rather than simply exercising their general function or preserving the peace and upholding the law.'[75] Police have performed the same blacklegging function in subsequent ambulance crew disputes. Gillian Morris points out that this use of the police raises several legal problems, not least that of whether or not the police disciplinary codes can force police officers to blackleg.[76]

References

1. E.C.S. Wade and G.G. Phillips, *Constitutional and Administrative Law* (1977), p.506.
2. Geoffrey Marshall, 'The Armed Forces and Industrial Disputes in the United Kingdom', in *Armed Forces and Society* (February 1979), p.271.
3. See V.I. Allen, *Trade Unions and the Government* (1960), p.118. Other works covering the use of troops in strikes in the 19th century include J.I. and B. Hammond, *The Skilled Labourer* (1919) and A. Aspinall, *The Early English Trade Unions* (1949).
4. Report of the Committee of Inquiry into the Disturbances at Featherstone, Parliamentary Papers, Vol.XVIII (1893).
5. Tony Hayter, *The Army and the Crowd in Mid-Georgian England* (1978), p.3.
6. See, e.g., Robert Rizzi, 'The British Army and Riot Control in Early 19th Century England' in *Army Quarterly* (January 1979), p.74.
7. Esther Moir, *The Justice of the Peace* (1969), p.10.
8. *Ibid.*, p.177.
9. *The Queen's Regulations for the Army*, third edition (1844), p.209.
10. *Ibid.*
11. Evidence of Richard Haldane, Secretary of State for War, Select Committee on the Employment of the Military in Cases of Disturbances (1908), p.11.
12. *Ibid.*, p.8.
13. *Ibid.*, p.11.
14. *Ibid.*, p.iii.
15. *Hansard*, 5 March 1908.
16. 1908 Select Committee, *op. cit.*, p.13.
17. Criminal Law Act 1967, s.3(1).

18. J.C. Smith and Brian Hogan, *Criminal Law* (1978), p.324.
19. *Ibid.,* p.327. See also, Michael Supperstone, *Brownlie's Law of Public Order and National Security* (1981) p.135.
20. *Manual of Military Law* Part II (1968), p.509.
21. *Hansard,* 22 August 1911, col. 2286.
22. 1908 Select Committee, *op. cit.,* p.v.
23. A.L. Morton, *A People's History of England* (1965), p.510.
24. *British Labour Statistics: Historical Abstract 1886-1968,* Department of Employment (1971).
25. Robin Evelegh, *Peace-keeping in a Democratic Society* (1978) p.16.
26. *Ibid.*
27. Randolph Churchill, *Winston Churchill,* vol.2 (1967), p.379.
28. *The Times,* 23 August 1911.
29. *Hansard,* 22 August 1911, col.2327.
30. *Ibid.,* col.2286.
31. *Ibid.,* col.2328.
32. *The Times,* 18 August 1911.
33. *Hansard,* 22 August 1911, col.2286.
34. *The Times,* 28 August 1911.
35. *Hansard,* 22 August 1911, col.2335.
36. *Ibid.,* col.2340.
37. Keith Jeffery and Peter Hennessy, *States of Emergency* (1983), p.6.
38. *Ibid.,* p.7.
39. *Ibid.,* p.9.
40. *Hansard,* 10 April 1917, col.1309.
41. CAB 28/74, 5 March 1920.
42. *Ibid.*
43. *Ibid.*
44. Memorandum by the Chairman of the Supply and Transport Committee, CAB 24/108, CP1575.
45. Memorandum by the Chairman of the Home Affairs Committee to the Cabinet, CAB 24/109, CP1559.
46. See Henry Pelling, *A History of British Trade Unionism* (1971), p.164.
47. Gillian S. Morris, 'The Emergency Powers Act 1920' in *Public Law* (Winter 1979), p.318. See Tony Bunyan, *The Political Police in Britain* (1977) for the background to the passing of the Act.
48. *Hansard,* 20 February 1964, col.1420.
49. *Hansard,* 25 November 1920, col.1399.
50. Emergency Powers Act 1920, s.1(1).
51. *Ibid.,* s.2(1).
52. CAB 24/109 CP 1659, 21 July 1920.
53. G.S. Morris, *op. cit.,* p.321.
54. *Ibid.,* p.333.
55. Jeffery and Hennessy, *op. cit.,* p.140.
56. *Ibid.,* p.141.
57. *The Times,* 30 May 1919.
58. *Daily Herald,* 19 May 1919.
59. *TUC Annual Report,* 1919, p.325.
60. Quoted in Jeffery and Hennessy, *op. cit.,* p.23; their book is an invaluable account of the post-1918 administrative history of contingency planning.
61. *Ibid.,* p.38.
62. CAB 24/161 CP 314(23).
63. Jeffery and Hennessy, *op. cit.,* p.85; see pp.76-87 for a full history of the Labour government and the difficulties it experienced with emergency planning.

64. *Hansard,* 3 May 1926, col.71.
65. CAB 24/174 CP390(25).
66. Margaret Morris, *The General Strike* (1976), p.158; see pp.150-64 for a more detailed study of these plans, and the whole book for an account of the General Strike itself.
67. *Ibid.,* p.164.
68. *Ibid.*
69. *Ibid.,* p.256.
70. C.G. Grey, *A History of the Air Ministry* (1940).
71. *The Times,* 16 November 1979.
72. Brian Bond, *British Military Policy between the Two World Wars* (1980), p.91.
73. Jeffery and Hennessy, *op. cit.,* p.119.
74. Bond, *op. cit.,* p.91.
75. Gillian S. Morris, 'The Police and Industrial Emergencies' in *Industrial Law Journal* (March 1980), p.1.
76. *Ibid.,* pp.1-12.

Two

1939-1983: The Law and the Machinery

At the outbreak of the Second World War, an emergency regulation was passed to enable troops to be used in agricultural work if there was an urgent need for their assistance under the difficult conditions of wartime. It is this regulation which remains the standard mechanism for deploying troops in strikes, except on the now rare occasions when a state of emergency is declared under the Emergency Powers Act 1920.

Regulation Six was made under the Emergency Powers (Defence) Act 1939 and was subsequently renewed and continued in force by a succession of temporary acts until it was made permanent by a further Emergency Powers Act in 1964. Just what powers the 1964 Act gives the government, however, is the subject of considerable confusion, as it is now being used for a purpose for which it was never designed and its wording is ambiguous.

From the 1939 Regulation to the 1964 Act

The 1939 Act was passed in late August 1939 to give Chamberlain's National government extensive powers during the coming war. Regulation Six was made under section 1 of the Act on 28 September and amended in 1942 to the following form, which remained in force until 1959:

'The Admiralty, the Army Council or the Air Council may by order authorise officers and men of His Majesty's Naval, Military or Air Forces under their respective control to be temporarily employed in agricultural work or such other work as may be approved in accordance with instructions issued by the Admiralty, the Army Council or the Air Council, as the case may be *as being urgent work of national importance,* and thereupon it shall be the duty of every person subject to the Naval Discipline Act, military law or the Air Force Act to obey

51

any command given by his superior officer in relation to such employment, and every such command shall be deemed to be a lawful command within the meaning of the Naval Discipline Act, the Army Act or the Air Force Act, as the case may be.' (Author's emphasis).

The original 1939 version of Regulation Six applied only to agricultural work; the words 'or such other work as may be approved' were added in 1942.

After the war ended, Regulation Six was continued in force by the Emergency Laws (Transitional Provisions) Act 1946, the Emergency Laws (Miscellaneous Provisions) Act 1947, the various Emergency Laws (Continuance) Orders and the Emergency Laws (Repeal) Act 1959 (Schedule 2, Part C). The 1959 Act slightly altered the wording (but not the meaning) by inserting the date '1955' after both 'the Army Act' and 'the Air Force Act' at the end of the last sentence, thereby bringing the regulation into line with the most recent legislation.

The 1959 Act extended the life of Regulation Six to the end of 1964 and, in June of that year, the Conservative Government made the regulation permanent in its 1959 form in section 2 of the Emergency Powers Act 1964.

The only other section of the 1964 Act, s.1, slightly broadened the scope of the Emergency Powers Act 1920 to provide for non-human agencies justifying the proclaiming of a state of emergency. In section 1(1) of the 1920 Act the words from 'any action' to 'extensive a scale' were replaced by the words 'there have occurred, or are about to occur, events of such a nature', so that the section now reads:

'If at any time it appears to His Majesty that there have occurred, or are about to occur, events of such a nature as to be calculated, by interfering with the supply and distribution of food, water, fuel or light, or with the means of locomotion, to deprive the community, or any substantial portion of the community, of the essentials of life, His Majesty may, by proclamation . . . declare that a state of emergency exists'.

References to the Admiralty, Army Council and Air Council are now construed as being to the Defence Council, and references to the various Acts as being to the Acts that have replaced them.

The wording of s.2 of the Emergency Powers Act 1964 is the same as that of the 1939 Defence Regulation Six as amended in 1942. The way it has been used however, is very different.

52

Parliament originally agreed to the Regulation on the understanding that it was being passed to cope with the perils of war. Nevertheless, since 1945 governments have utilised it for quite another purpose: to use troops to replace striking workers.

What 'emergency powers' does the 1964 Act actually give today's governments?

To the onlooker unaware of the long and difficult history of the legal basis of military intervention in strikes, this law might seem quite straightforward. The first part of section 2 of this Act quoted above (down to 'national importance') can be, and often is, taken to mean that the 1964 Act in itself *gives* the government the power to use troops temporarily in 'urgent work of national importance'; the definition of which can, not unreasonably be extended to include strikes in essential industries. In its second part, from the words 'and thereupon it shall be' to the end, the 1964 Act legalises the orders given to the troops engaged on such work and brings them within the scope of the military discipline laws (primarily the Army Act 1955, the Air Force Act 1955 and the Naval Discipline Act 1957).

If it did not do so, individual service personnel could refuse to obey those orders as the work was not 'military' as defined by those Acts.

The 1964 Act could, therefore, easily be interpreted as resolving finally two very thorny problems for governments. It could be interpreted first, as overriding the possible common law power of the magistrates to requisition troops by giving national government that right, and, second, as defining strike-breaking as a military activity covered by the discipline acts.

In fact, the Act appears originally to have been intended only to cover the latter of those two issues, the legality of the orders. In recent correspondence with the author, the Ministry of Defence has indeed confirmed that it still considers this to be the *only* interpretation of the Act. i.e. that the sole effect of the 1964 Act is to legalise the orders given to troops. The first part of s.2 of the 1964 Act is, the MoD claims, simply a re-statement of a Royal Prerogative power to deploy troops at will inside Britain: 'The deployment of the Armed Forces' it writes, 'is a matter for the Crown, and the 1964 Act has no bearing on this.'[1]

The Royal Prerogative

It is by no means certain, however, that this Royal Prerogative power does actually exist. The Royal Prerogative is 'the residue of discretionary or arbitrary authority which at any given time is legally left in the hands of the crown.'[2] In the Middle Ages, the crown had very extensive powers, including that of supreme command of the army, which it still retains. Few of these administrative powers over the military have expressly been removed from the crown; instead, their execution has been taken over by government ministers who, through their accountability to Parliament, are considered to embody the principle of democratic parliamentary control over the armed forces. Hence, the Royal Prerogative still plays an important role in the running of the armed forces and their relationship with the civil population. But just how far the prerogative extends is, according to some academics in the field, an 'interesting but obscure question'.[3]

Successive governments have, not surprisingly perhaps, favoured a wide definition of the extent of the prerogative. This interpretation is supported by a substantial body of legal opinion, best exemplified, perhaps, by Lord Reid's statement in the House of Lords that: 'It is in my opinion clear that the disposition and armament of the armed forces, are and for centuries have been, within the exclusive discretion of the crown.'[4]

If this Royal Prerogative power *does* exist in this form — and governments have been acting as though it does since at least 1964 — then it raises a number of important political and constitutional issues. First, the decisions to use troops can be, and are, taken by ministers and their advisers, senior military officers and civil servants without *any* involvement by parliament, despite the fact that these have often been major decisions of public policy (just one example being the Fire Brigades Union's challenge to government pay policies in 1977 and its failure after prolonged military deployment). The only major formality that the government has to fulfil to implement the prerogative is that not less than two members of the Defence Council have to sign an order under the Emergency Powers Act 1964 (see below), a move which has usually been made without any publicity. All the other steps taken to mobilise the troops are made in the privacy of Whitehall.

Secondly, the centralisation into a few hands of this power to deploy the military has contributed to the secrecy which surrounds contingency planning in which only recently a few peepholes have developed. This secrecy has concealed the true extent of military mobilisations, thereby disguising just how involved the armed forces have become in British industrial conflict — a level of involvement the military consistently claims it neither has, nor wants. Whether or not secrecy was intentional, and whether or not the armed forces wanted their existing role in industrial disputes, the British state now possesses a sophisticated planning apparatus that can mobilise thousands of troops to intervene in a wide range of civilian strikes and almost guarantee to reduce their effectiveness. The lack of democratic involvement in major questions concerning the armed forces is officially justified by claims that such decisions fall within the scope of the Royal Prerogative.

The Role of Magistrates in Strikes

If this Royal Prerogative power to deploy troops in strikes does not exist, the government may have no authority, other than the Emergency Powers Act 1920 (by declaring a state of emergency) to use troops in strikes. The existence of the prerogative in this case is questionable because the common law (of which the prerogative is a part) may in fact give the power to mobilise troops to the magistrates, not the government.

The common law is 'the unwritten law . . . which does not derive its authority from any express declaration of the will of the legislature. This unwritten law has the same force and effect as statute law. . . . It receives its binding power from long and immemorial usage and universal reception throughout the realm.'[5] The Royal Prerogative is part of the common law but 'the sovereign can claim no prerogatives except such as the law allows, nor such as are contrary to Magna Carta or any other statute, or to the liberties of the subject.'[6]

Underlying the Ministry of Defence's argument that it has an inherited blanket Royal Prerogative power to deploy troops as it wishes is the fact that parliament has never removed any such power from the scope of the prerogative. But this does not prove that the power existed in the first place. The other side of the argument is that up until comparatively recently it was widely understood that the prerogative did not extend to the internal deployment of the military against the civilian population and that the common law in fact said that such deployments had to be directed by the magistrates.

As we have seen above (pages 19-23), from the time of the establishment of the standing army in the mid-17th century until the First World War, opposition to the use of the military inside Britain, and very poor national communications, obliged the crown to recognise that it was neither politically advisable nor technically possible to mobilise troops by itself against civilians. Between the middle of the 18th century and the First World War, the government was thus forced to rely on a local 'civil authority', the magistracy, to manage the internal deployment of military forces.

By the time the serious disturbances of 1911 occurred, this position had widely become understood as being part of the common law. If this was the common law position at that time, then the common law today could still be that the magistrates, mayors and sheriffs, and not the government, have the power to call out the troops, as there has been no change in statute law since that time. In this case, governments could have used troops illegally to break up to 30 strikes since 1945.

Can this locally-based procedure in fact be said to have been a part of common law? There are a number of arguments *against* this. First, that this pre-First World War method of calling out troops only applied to riotous disturbances and that using troops to replace striking workers is a new phenomenon not covered by any previous common law; thus it comes under the Royal Prerogative. Secondly, it can be said that the requirement to consult a 'civil authority' was a self-imposed duty, an administrative convenience for the government, who must by definition be the final civil authority. Under this argument, government could appoint the magistrates (or anybody else) as their 'deputy' civil authorities, but then remove them at will if the final legal control over the internal deployment of troops does still lie in the Royal Prerogative. Thirdly, no legal 'authority' in the strict sense of the word, accepts the magistrate-based procedure as law.

The arguments supporting the assertion that the magistrates-based procedure *is* part of common law (and therefore in conflict with the prerogative power) are, first, that immediately before the First World War everybody, strikers, employers, the government, the legal profession and the public at large, seemed to believe that it was. If this were not the position, then the government (who had most to gain) could have been relied upon to say so; it did not. Even in 1934, the government of the day was not aware that it had any ancient prerogative power to intervene; as Duff Cooper, Financial Secretary to the War Office, said during the parliamentary debate on the renewing of the Army and Air Force (Annual) Act 'We [the government] do not pretend that we have any right to make use of troops in order to interfere with an industrial dispute. We do not believe that we have any legal right to attempt to break a strike by using troops to carry out duties which, in normal times, would be carried out by civilians.'[7] And new prerogative powers cannot be invented. Hood Phillips says: 'Since the prerogative is part of common law, the Queen cannot claim that a new prerogative has come into existence. It can only be the residue at any given time of the rights and powers which the sovereign had before the days of parliament.'[8]

Secondly, we know that recent governments have agreed that in the related area of public order, the magistrates-based system does have validity, because attempts have only recently been made to change it. This is significant because, before the First World War, the Liberal government's own Select Committee into the Employment of the Military in Cases of Disturbances implicitly agreed that the term 'disturbances' covered ordinary strikes. Only a court of law could now settle whether or not the law relating to public order, which certainly used to be applied partially to military intervention in strikes, does still apply, because for decades now governments have followed separate practices that assume that it no longer does so.

The Role of Magistrates in Public Order

Until 1973, governments accepted the traditional common law view that the magistrates-based system applied in periods of disorder. Until 1973, the Queen's Regulations for the Army stated, as they had done since 1844 (and had been recommended practice for the military for 80 years before then) that troops should only be mobilised in aid of the civil power on the requisition of a magistrate. (Or, more precisely, in the counties by a county magistrate, in towns and cities the mayor, in London the Metropolitan Police Commissioner and in Scotland the Sheriffs). The system, as it existed in 1973, had first appeared in outline around 1730. The government made it the recommended procedure for the military about 1760 and it became codified in the Queen's Regulations in 1844.[9]

Troops responding to the magistrate's requisition were under only the same legal obligations as other citizens. The magistrates, being the civil power, could under the common law call on *all* citizens to come to their aid in suppressing disturbances. Troops answering this call had no special rights or privileges; they were (and are) in that context only a section of the citizenry.

In September 1973, however, the Heath government changed the two-centuries-old procedure, quietly and unannounced. The internal disturbances of 1970-72 had shown that, for the first time since the 1926 General Strike, troops might have to be requisitioned for public order duties. Following a review of all emergency plans, the government amended the Queen's Regulations in order to centralise all public order duties under the police and the Home Office.

References to the 'civil authority' were dropped from the Regulations which now say that military assistance 'will normally be requested by the Chief Officer of Police' (i.e. the Chief

Constable, or Metropolitan Commissioner). Where the request comes from a 'source other than the Chief Officer of Police' the Chief Constable has to be consulted before any action is taken.[10]

Did the government have the power to change the Regulations, thereby fundamentally changing the relationship between civil and military power by taking the authority to mobilise troops away from the locally based (and in the towns, democratically accountable) figures to give it to senior police officers who are answerable to nobody in operational matters? This question, again, is probably only resolvable in the courts. The answer will once more hinge on whether a centuries-old mechanism for settling a problem (public order) has been part of common law, or whether only the general principles underlying that mechanism — the citizen's obligations in that disorder — are embodied in the law.

The degree of confusion surrounding this issue (and some of the thinking underlying the 1973 change) can be seen in a statement by one of the key figures involved in this redefinition of the civil power, Robert Mark, then Commissioner of the Metropolitan Police. In his book *Policing a Perplexed Society* Mark writes that military assistance 'was formerly sought by police from the magistracy rather than the Home Office, but *whatever the legal position,* present practice reflects the emergence of a professional, well-organised police service which has inevitably assumed the primary responsibility for law and order.'[11] (Author's emphasis).

The relationship between the use of the magistrate-based procedure for public order problems and for strike-breaking needs to be clarified. As we have seen, these two activities were considered synonymous before World War One, but this is no longer the case and the distinction between the two activities has been emphasised by the military's own quite separate definition of them, Military Aid to the Civil Power (MACP) and Military Aid to the Civil Ministries (MACM).

Modern governments do in fact accept that some other body should first ask for troops before they are mobilised and occasionally this body is still called the 'civil authority'. As Defence Secretary Francis Pym said in 1980, 'The Defence Council would not authorise such employment unless it was so requested by the civil authority.'[12] But governments no longer appear to see this as a *legal* requirement, rather as an administrative one which both softens their public image and eases the actual process of identifying and dealing with problematic strikes. Moreover, this 'civil authority' is no longer considered to be the magistrates but usually the employing organisation whose workforce is on strike, backed up by the government department covering that employer's area of work.

We are left with a basic question: was the magistrates-based procedure for mobilising troops a part of common law or only an administrative device for implementing the Royal Prerogative? Legal opinion currently appears to tend towards the latter view, but the problem has not been seriously addressed. This question (and the ones that preceded it) are so important and legally complex that they should be resolved in a court, the only forum capable of deciding what is the common law. If the procedure were shown to be an extant part of common law, then the government's power to break strikes unilaterally 'in the national interest' would be undermined. Furthermore, if deteriorating economic conditions should lead to military intervention in strikes once again becoming a cause of rioting and disorder, then the relevance of the case for the magistrates-based procedure would become even stronger.

The Meaning of the 1964 Act

We now need to return to the 1964 Act to consider its exact meaning in the light of the above.

It will be remembered that the 1964 Act has two components: first, a restatement of the (disputed) prerogative power to deploy troops on non-military work; second, provisions legalising the orders given to troops engaged on that work.

It must first of all be asked whether the 1964 Act has any meaning at all if the magistrates-based procedure *is* part of the present law. If the prerogative power restated in the Act does not in fact exist, does this invalidate the meaning of the Act? If this were found to be the case then no government would be able to use troops for national strike-breaking (except in the limited circumstances of the 1920 Act) and, were they to do so, orders given to the troops would not be lawful. The government would have to rely on local magistrates to decide whether or not to mobilise the military.

Alternatively, it is possible that despite the MoD's assertion to the contrary, the ambiguity of the 1964 Act is such that it 'unintentionally' turns the prerogative power to deploy troops (even if it had never previously existed) into statute law. Thereby it would render any contemporary discussion of the role of the magistrates unnecessary. Although this may be one interpretation of the 1964 Act, it was not parliament's intention that this should be so.

If this last interpretation of the law is correct, or, alternatively, if the government does have the disputed prerogative power, then the 1964 Act does legalise the orders given to blacklegging troops. But here another problem arises, because the restatement of the prerogative power in the Act limits the work that troops may be ordered to undertake to 'urgent work of national importance'.[13] Since 1945, however, the *majority* of the strikes that troops have intervened in have *not* been national disputes, only affecting certain parts of the country (in some cases only one town or city).

Before exploring this particular issue further, it is necessary to ask whether it is the prerogative itself, or the summary of it in a statute, which has legal effect. This is crucial because, if the original prerogative is superior to statute law, then the government does not have to consider itself limited by the question of 'national importance' as the prerogative itself appears to have no such limitation attached to it. The Ministry of Defence prefers this latter interpretation of the law, under which it would have much wider powers than it would under the wording of s.2 of the 1964 Act, and powers that could not be challengeable in the courts. Only the *existence* of a prerogative power can be inquired into by a court, not the way the prerogative is exercised.[14] According to Hood Philips, however: 'An Act may be passed covering the same ground as the prerogative, in which case the prerogative is to that extent by necessary implication abrogated.'[15]

If this principle can be applied to this rather unusual case or, if the 1964 Act does intentionally turn the prerogative into statute, then we are left with a clear clash between the law and government practice: i.e. governments, since the end of the Second World War, have been acting *ultra vires* by using troops to break strikes that have not been of 'national importance'. And when similar situations arise in the future, as they almost certainly will, troops ordered to carry out this strike-breaking could refuse to do so, as the work may not be covered by the military discipline laws.

When the 1964 Act was summarised in the Army Regulations, a further problem arose over this question of 'national importance'. Until 1978, the Regulations stated that 'where there is no proclamation [of a state of emergency] and the emergency is limited and local' troops may be used on 'urgent work of national importance'.[16] But how could the emergency be 'limited and local' and at the same time involve work of 'national importance'? This contradiction was first pointed out (by the author and another member of the State Research group, Tony Bunyan) after troops had taken over the whole fire service during the 1977 national fire brigades strike, clearly not a 'limited and local' dispute.[17] Service personnel had been ordered to intervene in a nationwide dispute in clear breach of their own Regulations.

Although the Army Regulations have no standing in law, the Callaghan Government was then in a politically embarrassing position. The drafters of the 1939 Defence Regulation had intended the measure simply to legalise orders in agricultural and similar emergencies that might occur in wartime. At that time 'limited and local' emergencies could also involve work of 'national importance' and the world 'limited and local' had presumably been retained in the post-war Army Regulations because they expressed the intention of the 1939 Regulation. The drafters of the Regulation had not intended that it would be used in national strikes which, in the 1930s, were seen as covered by the Emergency Powers Act 1920, and it appears that the authors of the Army Regulations were aware of this and inserted the words to explain their meaning.

The governments of the 1970s however, wanted to use the 1964 Act to deal with strikes. The Callaghan government was trying to avoid declaring a state of emergency for industrial disputes and the wording of the 1964 Act appears to have been interpreted as providing just enough legal cover to allow the government to use it. As a Ministry of Defence spokesperson told the author shortly after the fire brigades strike ended, however, the words 'limited and local' in the (then) current Regulations had been 'inadvertently retained from earlier Regulations', providing an embarrassing reminder of the way the law should have been employed. On 1 June 1978, therefore, the government removed the words 'limited and local' from the Queen's Regulations in a belated attempt to fit a legal square peg into a round hole, while at the same time leaving the way open for troops to be used in future in strikes of national importance; again, not the intention of the original law at all.

Whatever the precise meaning of the 1964 Act it should be noted that the 'order' given by the Defence Council to authorise military intervention is technically a Defence Council Order and not an Order in Council. The distinction is important because an Order in Council (i.e. the Privy Council) has to be laid before Parliament and receive MPs' assent, if only in the negative sense of not being opposed. An Order in Council therefore provides MPs and the public with an opportunity both to find out what the government is doing and to take some action in relation to it if desired.

Defence Council Orders, on the other hand, are executive instruments of the Defence Council, the MoD's administrative body that comprises ministers, senior officers and top civil servants. Defence Council Orders are neither published nor laid before parliament. Orders mobilising troops to intervene in major strikes therefore can be — and usually are — made and imple-mented without anyone outside the military knowing anything about them.

The Law — a Summary

In summary, the legal position on the use of troops in strikes looks like this. Only one thing is certain: in the most serious emergencies the government can declare a state of emergency under the Emergency Powers Act 1920 and then give itself wide-ranging authority over the direction and control of society, including using troops to break strikes (see chapter one).

Beyond this, the position is unclear. The government believes that it has a Royal Prerogative power to deploy troops as it wishes inside Britain and that it therefore needs no further legal authority to break strikes. It sees the sole purpose of the only other relevant statute, the Emergency Powers Act 1964, as being to legalise the orders given to troops engaged on strike-breaking. This is the simplest interpretation of the law and the most convenient for the government but it is questionable on several grounds.

First, it is by no means certain that the prerogative power exists as, in common law, local magistrates, mayors and Scottish sheriffs may be the appropriate civil authorities for mobilising troops, not the government. If this is the case, then governments since 1945 have been acting *ultra vires* and future national direction of military strike-breaking would be almost impossible, without amending the legislation.

Secondly, however, the uncertain wording of the 1964 Act may unintentionally bestow on the government this prerogative power to mobilise troops in statutory form if it does not already possess it. Alternatively, the government may have actually possessed this wide (disputed) power, but this may have been abrogated by the more limited 1964 Act. Legal opinion currently tends to the view that governments do possess the prerogative power in some form, although this is far from certain because the issue has never been directly considered by the courts.

If the government's power to mobilise troops does take one of the above statutory forms (rather than the pure prerogative forms) then governments since 1945 will have used troops illegally to break strikes for a different reason: because the 1964 Act states that troops can only be used on 'urgent work of national importance' and many of the post-1945 disputes have not fallen into this category. In local strikes in the future individual members of the armed services could refuse to obey orders, as the government will have acted *ultra vires* by mobilising the troops and the orders given to them will therefore not be lawful.

If the government does possess the prerogative power in its pure (non-statutory) form, then the problem over 'urgent work of national importance' will not be so much legal as moral, for governments will only be acting against the spirit of the 1964 Act rather than actually breaking it.

The Politics of the Law

Confusion over the precise meaning of the law relating to military intervention in strikes also has important political implications.

First, the unquestioning acceptance for most of the post-1945 years of the government's legal right to intervene in strikes has helped to establish a general political climate markedly less hostile to military intervention in British civilian affairs than was the case in the past.

Secondly, successive governments' claims to a Royal Prerogative power to send in the troops has removed the issue from effective parliamentary scrutiny. MPs have no right to prior discussion, or even knowledge, of proposed government interventions and have even been denied accurate statistics regarding past interventions, as, for example, in the Written Answer from the Defence Secretary to Robin Cook MP[18] which omits nearly a third of post-1945 interventions, amongst other errors.

The passing of the 1964 Emergency Powers Bill through parliament did, however, give the country's elected representatives an extremely rare chance to discuss the subject of emergency powers in general and the use of troops in strikes in particular.[19] Unfortunately, this opportunity for democratic influence over one of the most contentious areas of government policy was largely wasted as the government gave the Labour opposition almost no warning of the contents of the Bill. Consequently the discussion was largely unprepared and uninformed. Some Labour MPs did voice their general opposition to the introduction of new emergency powers and questioned why they were being introduced at that moment. As Sidney Silverman MP, the most vocal opponent of the Bill, said: 'It is not necessary to give the government all sorts of tyrannical powers in anticipation of academic possibilities not even described to the House. What has become of our parliamentary democracy? Where are we getting to?'; while former Home Secretary Chuter Ede commented: 'The more power a government gets in this kind of relationship the more difficult it is to restrain some people from wanting to put the power into practice.'[21]

The government did not make it clear when it introduced the Bill that it would become an anti-strike weapon. Home Secretary Henry Brooke mentioned that the 1939 Regulation had helped in 'maintaining essential supplies'[22] and then went on to say: 'I think that the Bill as a whole is a wise exercise in foresight. It is an insurance policy against contingencies — remote contingencies, perhaps, but real ones nevertheless.'[23] Brooke left it to his audience to guess what these remarks might mean when translated into practice. He and his Cabinet colleagues have since been accused on many occasions of deliberately misleading parliament and the country as to the real purpose of the 1964 Act.

The real distortion of parliament's intention, however, took place perhaps when the 1939 Regulation was first passed and then amended in 1942; in those early days Regulation Six was clearly only aimed at agricultural and similar *natural* emergencies. Its meaning was first subverted by the 1945 Labour government. As C.M. Woodhouse, Under-Secretary of State at the Home Office, pointed out during the 1964 debate: 'Clause two gives permanent status to temporary provisions which have not in practice proved controversial in operation and whose periodical renewal has never been contested.'[24] But wherever the responsibility lies, one thing is certain: the 1964 Act had its origin in a desire by parliament to mitigate the effects of natural disasters; parliament never intended that the measure should become the state's second line of defence in strikes, complementing the Emergency Powers Act 1920. Governments since 1945 have used a law for a purpose for which it was never intended.

None of these issues concerned the public when Defence Regulation Six was passed in the autumn of 1939, as no one could foresee that a law brought in to deal with the grave and exceptional circumstances of war would find a new and very important role in peacetime against a different enemy: strikers. But military black-legging was also to be a much less controversial issue after 1945 than any pre-war contingency planner could have forseen and the question of the legitimacy of such strike-breaking has seldom been raised in the post-war decades, as will be seen in the chronology of military interventions in strikes from 1945 that follows in chapters three to five.

Given the complexity of the law, it is not possible to say with precision whether or not each of the 36 military interventions detailed in the chronology were legal, but question marks hang over the great majority of them. Even in the six cases where states of emergency were declared and troops used, it is by no means certain that three of the emergencies concerned were sufficiently serious to warrant the use of the 1920 Act.

With the other 30 interventions it is perhaps most instructive to assume that the government does have some form of right to intervene based on the 1964 Act, and then to ask which mobilisations have fallen within that Act's criterion of 'urgent work of national importance', as with this phrase parliament was presumably expressing some intention to limit the otherwise potentially very extensive power of the government. In these words legal and political fears come together.

The problem here is one of definitions. In one sense all the 1945-50 interventions, except that at Buckingham Palace in 1948

1. *Police, cavalry and soldiers with fixed bayonets escort a convoy past a strikers meeting in Liverpool in 1911.* (Press Association).

2. *Soldiers camped out in Kensington Gardens in preparation for the 1921 coal strike.* (BBC Hulton Picture Library).

*3. A young soldier gives two people a lift to work during a
transport strike in the 1920s. (BBC Hulton Picture Library).*

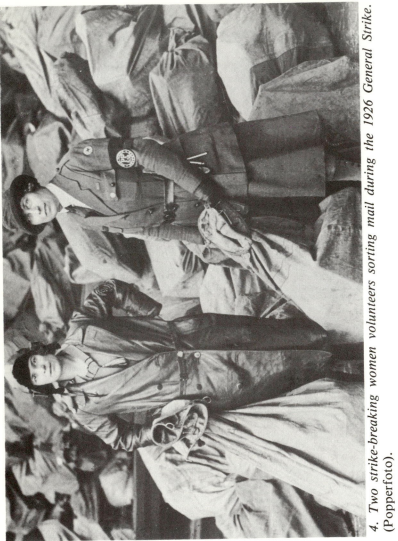

4. *Two strike-breaking women volunteers sorting mail during the 1926 General Strike.* (Popperfoto).

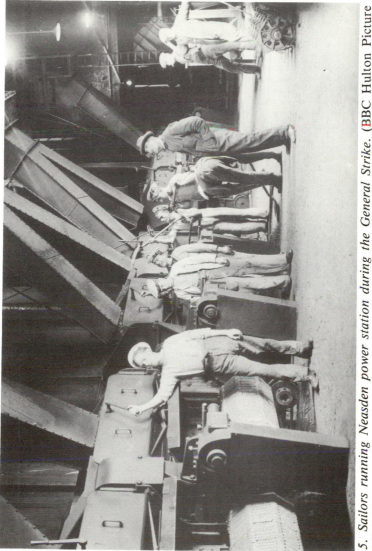

5. *Sailors running Neasden power station during the General Strike.* (BBC Hulton Picture Library).

6. *January 1947: striking workers at Smithfield meat market watch Guardsmen shift carcasses.* (BBC Hulton Picture Library).

7. *Soldiers settling in at the Clapham Deep Tube Shelter under
Clapham Common, their base for operations during the January
1947 Smithfield strike.* (Associated Press).

8. *The 1949 dock strike: troops unloading meat from the* Argentina Star *in the Royal Victoria Docks, London.* (BBC Hulton Picture Library).

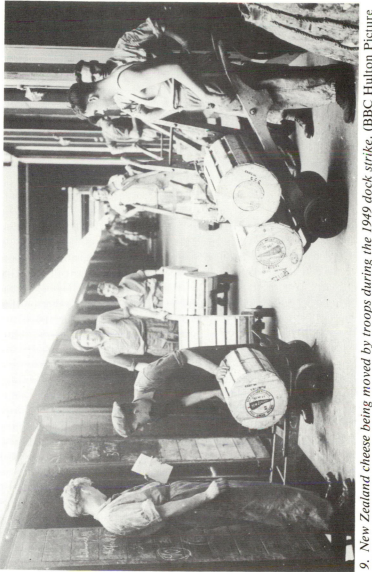

9. *New Zealand cheese being moved by troops during the 1949 dock strike.* (BBC Hulton Picture Library).

10. *October 1953: soldiers marching from Waterloo station to Woolwich in readiness for the imminent petrol tanker drivers strike.* (Popperfoto).

11. Troops filling a petrol tanker in Poplar during the 1953 tanker drivers strike. (BBC Hulton Picture Library).

12. *The Royal Navy to the rescue during the 1966 seamens strike: 'essential supplies' being delivered to the Western Isles of Scotland.* (Popperfoto).

13. *Grenadier Guards clearing rubbish in Tower Hamlets during the 1970 local authority manual workers strike.* (BBC Hulton Picture Library).

14. *The 1977 fire brigades strike: soldiers fight a major fire in an industrial estate in East London.* (Press Association).

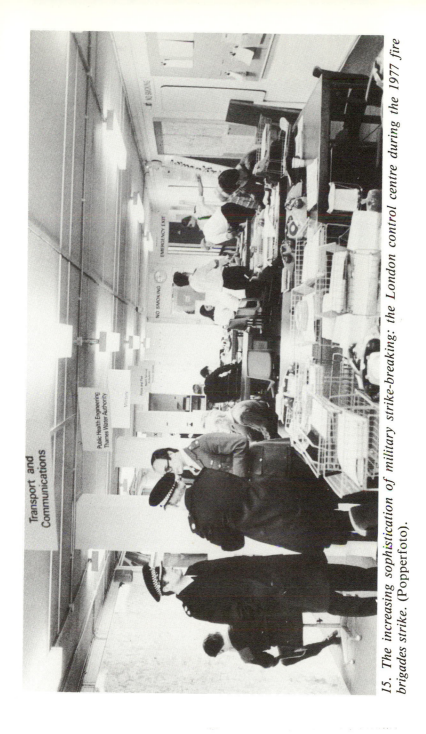

15. *The increasing sophistication of military strike-breaking: the London control centre during the 1977 fire brigades strike.* (Popperfoto).

16. *A London ambulance officer shows troops how to carry a stretcher in readiness for the 1979 ambulance crews strike.* (Popperfoto).

which was only urgent and important to the Royal Family, were 'urgent work of national importance', as the country was still effectively operating under wartime economic conditions. Then, even relatively minor disputes, especially in the docks, could threaten the health and well-being of large sections of the public. But on the other hand the public was not threatened at a *national* level by all these strikes, and it could be argued that the law did not cover the essentially local strikes in the docks in early 1945, 1946, 1947 and 1950, at Smithfield in 1946 and 1950, Tower Bridge in 1947, London power stations in 1949 and London gas works in 1950.

The same doubts can be raised about the London oil tanker drivers strike in 1953, by which time the economy had recovered, and by the 1960 seamens strike, although this latter intervention was generally accepted as an humanitarian move rather than as strike-breaking.

Since 1970 military intervention in non-national strikes in the public sector has become a regular feature of government pay policies and the question of its lawfulness therefore becomes more pressing. Troops were used 16 times between 1970 and the 1983 general election outside of states of emergency. The 1980 prison officers' dispute was handled by new and unusual legislation, leaving 15 interventions coming under the contentious 1964 Act. The only one of these which was clearly 'urgent work of national importance' was the 1977 national fire brigades strike; the other 14 are more open to question.

The Ministry of Defence argues that the five cases where troops took over military-type jobs in military establishments (naval dockyard disputes in 1978, 1979 and 1981, the industrial civil servants strike of 1979 and the seizure of the *Keren* in 1983) did not require any use of the 1964 Act as the work could be called 'military' and troops could therefore be ordered to carry it out in the ordinary course of their duties. The Ministry therefore did not issue orders under the Act on these occasions, or during a sixth dispute, the 1977 air traffic controllers strike, where the MoD said the civilian strikers were carrying out military work but the strikers strongly denied this. But with all six cases, if the work was actually military, why was it being performed by civilians? A definition of 'military work' needs to be found soon.

There are now eight interventions left to consider: 1970 Tower Hamlets refuse collectors, 1973 Glasgow fire brigade, 1975 Glasgow refuse collectors, 1979 ambulance crews and Westminster Hospital ancillary workers, 1981 and 1982 ambulance crews and 1982 railway workers. The most unusual and disturbing 1979 Westminster Hospital case is a clear instance of unlawful military action that should be investigated at once, particularly as there appears to be no record of it in the MoD. The other interventions — all maintaining essential services with greatly varying degrees of strike-breaking involved — were all 'urgent' but by no means of 'national' importance. These eight interventions could all be challenged as possibly falling outside the scope of the 1964 Act, and troops ordered to take part in them could have been able to refuse those orders.

The Machinery and the Planners

At the heart of the government's anti-strike system today lies the Civil Contingencies Unit.

The exact role and structure of this body have never been officially revealed, and even its very existence was still being formally denied in 1982, 10 years after it was set up. It has always been surrounded with great secrecy and most of the information that is known about it has come from press 'leaks'. Its primary purpose is to monitor and take action against strikes in key industries but its brief also takes in any other type of civil emergency, including hijackings and sieges, and it also has close links with the home defence structure.[25]

The CCU is the direct descendent of the contingency planning organisation that was developed in 1919-20 to meet the apparent threat of a working-class revolt. It continues the, by now, 'traditional' organisation of central emergency planning and decision making: a Cabinet sub-committee of ministers, which necessarily changes with each government, is supported by a standing body of senior officials, whose advice is normally followed by the ministers. This system has been shown in practice to give exceptional power to the officials in charge of its day-to-day operation.

The CCU was set up in 1972 following the miners strike early that year (see pages 116-7 for details). It is an almost infinitely flexible body, demonstrating an adaptability that has helped it succeed where a more rigid organisation would have disintegrated in failure. In time of industrial peace the CCU has shrunk to a handful of people, most notably its secretary and chairman, both Cabinet Office civil servants. The secretary is the key figure, responsible for maintaining the CCU's files and monitoring the industrial scene. When a problem appears, the secretary will ring the alarm bells that can result in the CCU swelling to a sizeable committee and operations unit, with representatives from all the major government departments, and meeting daily in major crises.

Former Home Secretary Merlyn Rees describes the CCU as being 'very *ad hoc*. There's a civil servant in the Cabinet Office who has a book with it all written in. If anything happens we in the Home Office would say, we'd better get the chap over and have a chat. He comes and we say "What shall we do — how long is the strike going to last?" He says, "I've been talking to union leaders X and Y and they say this and that" — we'd look at all the details. It's not a Home Office responsibility but we'd do it.' Rees confirms the influential position held by the civil servants: 'When a strike is looming you get in the department, have a meeting, discuss the problem, set tasks. If the civil servants had said to me [during the 1977-8 fire brigades strike, when he was Home Secretary] that we need a state of emergency to get the green goddesses [fire engines] then we would have had a state of emergency. I have always found the civil servants very good — I've no complaints.'[26]

The CCU alarm bells are most likely to be rung for disputes in industries providing 'essential' services: electricity, gas, water, sewerage, oil, health, fire brigades, ambulances, civilian-run defence work, coal, road transport and the docks. The majority of these are under some form of public control. Which industries are classified as 'essential' varies over time: the docks are now less important than they were following the development of large-scale air freighting, and the railways have become of less significance following the building of the motorway network.

The CCU is the focus of Whitehall contingency planning, employing the most experienced planners, who give advice to their colleagues in the government departments, and it is the place where all the threads of state contingency planning are pulled together. In emergencies, the CCU can use what Jeffery and Hennessy call 'the Cabinet Office's operations centre. . . Known in Whitehall as "COBRA" (Cabinet Office Briefing Room), it is fitted with a large round table around which the CCU ministers and officials sit. A cluster of microphones drop out of the ceiling and enable the Home Secretary, who chairs the committee whenever ministers are present, to speak directly with Chief Constables and major-generals in the military districts up and down the country.'[27]

The CCU has been located in the Cabinet Office, close to the Prime Minister, ever since contingency planning was taken away from the Home Office in 1972.

The precise constitutional position of the CCU is not altogether clear. In theory the officials who are advising the ministers and carrying out their orders should not be involved in the ministers' policy making. In practice, however, the ministers and officials work closely together at almost all levels, with ministers only meeting separately in the most serious crises. It appears that in non-emergency situations ministers and officials are effectively almost sharing policy-making, possibly a very efficient system administratively, but a rather disturbing one constitutionally. In fact, the name 'Civil Contingencies Unit' should strictly refer to the officials and their organisation, with another name being given to the Cabinet sub-committee it is supporting. The high level of secrecy surrounding both the names and composition of these Cabinet sub-committees, coupled with the closeness of the ministers and their CCU officials, has, however, led to this sub-committee also being referred to as the CCU, a source of considerable confusion.

The officials and ministers of the CCU can meet separately or together. When the more routine matters of contingency planning need to be discussed, the officials meet on their own. But if ministerial decisions need to be made the Home Secretary takes the chair and ministers from departments affected by the particular problem join in; the officials are then, technically, only advising their ministers. Separate meetings of ministers alone are convened only rarely, primarily when major strategic issues need to be resolved, as happened in the 1978-9 'Winter of Discontent'.

The mobilisation of troops for strike-breaking usually begins with a request from the strikers' employer, although in what the government sees as very serious disputes, such as the 1977 fire brigade strike (see page 130) the government will force troops on unwilling employers. The employers' request goes through the industry's 'sponsoring' department: all the important industries are 'sponsored', as the planners call it, by the government department with responsibility for their kind of work; the road transport industry, for example, is sponsored by the Department of Transport. All sponsoring departments now have their own emergency planning divisions, called by a confusing variety of names, that will initially examine the request for the military. The sponsor department, if it agrees with the proposal from the employers, then goes to the chief contingency planners at the CCU for further talks.

The Home Office is the sponsor department for certain services, such as the fire brigades, but also has a more general brief for monitoring what it calls all 'peacetime emergencies', as the Home Secretary has the primary responsibility for all internal security matters in Britain. This work is carried out by the Home Office's F6 (Emergency Services) Division, part of its Police Department. The other main responsibilities of F6, located in the main Home Office building in Queen Anne's Gate, are Home Defence and internal war plans.

The employer's request for troops, having reached the upper layers of Whitehall, would normally then be discussed at a CCU 'officials' meeting, which in turn would make a recommendation to a CCU ministerial meeting if action was thought to be necessary.

When a specific request for military assistance is being considered, ministers from the sponsoring department and the MoD (and the Welsh, Scottish and Northern Ireland Offices if they are affected) will be prominent in making the decision.

The decision to use troops would not normally go to the Cabinet. The process of MACM has now become so routine that the Cabinet is only very rarely involved (official sources say that *all* mobilisations of troops in 1980 and 1981 were authorised outside the Cabinet), unless a state of emergency is going to be declared. The contingency planning officials who run the CCU from day to day are, therefore, exercising a considerable influence over British trade unionists and industrial relations policy, as most decisions to use troops outside of an emergency are made in an administrative framework that the planners operate and in which they determine what information ministers shall have on which to base their decisions. For a disturbing example of the potential political power that the CCU planners can exert because of the way this system works, see the account of the 1977 Windscale industrial workers strike in chapter six (page 127).

Once it has been decided to mobilise troops, the legal framework in which to do it has to be settled. If possible, the contingency planners and ministers always try to avoid using the Emergency Powers Act 1920 and instead prefer to rely on the Royal Prerogative power (which they believe they have) to deploy troops around the country at governmental will. Before troops are mobilised, however, a Defence Council Order is signed by two members of the Defence Council, under the Emergency Powers Act 1964, to ensure that the orders given to the troops are lawful and, therefore, covered by the military discipline acts. If this order were not signed, individual soldiers could question the legality of the orders given to them by their commanding officers, as strike-breaking is not a military duty as prescribed in the discipline acts. The Defence Council is the policy-making body for the armed forces and consists of the Defence Ministers, senior civil servants and military officers.

If special powers are needed, to requisition vehicles, for example, then a state of emergency may have to be declared under the Emergency Powers Act 1920, and this will involve the CCU in producing coherent and convincing arguments that will stand up before the Cabinet, the Queen, parliament and the media. States of emergency are becoming rare as the system becomes more efficient; the last to be declared was during the miners strike of 1973-4 (see page 120).

Calling in the Troops

Having decided to use troops, the Minister of Defence has to instruct the Ministry of Defence itself to mobilise them. This order goes, first, through a Ministry of Defence division called Defence Secretariat Six. DS6 is part of the Ministry of Defence civilian-run administrative structure, controlled by an Assstant Secretary and coming under the Assistant Under-Secretary of State (General Staff). It is responsible for all army operational matters worldwide, including the use of troops on public order and strike-breaking roles inside Britain.

DS6, from its office in the Ministry of Defence's Main Building in Whitehall, authorises the army's operations command centre, the headquarters of United Kingdom Land Forces (UKLF) at Wilton near Salisbury, to arrange the deployment of troops. UKLF and DS6 will also have been consulted much earlier by the department and the other contingency planners to find out the Ministry of Defence's feelings on the particular request and to assess whether troops are actually available.

The RAF and Royal Navy provide personnel for strike-breaking alongside the army, but the army actually runs the MACM operations because it alone has the necessary regional and local administrative organisation. UKLF assesses which forces can be deployed and gives instructions to the RAF and Royal Navy and to the headquarters of the nine army districts into which Britain is divided (seven in England, plus Wales and Scotland). The district headquarters have operational control over all troops (army, Royal Navy and RAF) in their areas. The armed forces always maintain their own chains of command in strike-breaking actions, with military liaison officers providing the interface between them and the strike-hit employers.

The essence of the government strike-breaking system is its flexibility, and, when actually involved in MACM, the military, like the CCU, varies its procedures to meet the situation. Normally the military prefer to use their own vehicles, bases and communications, but in a major national strike where deployment in every locality and constant communication with civilian emergency services are necessary, then *ad hoc* arrangements are developed. If that experiment works, the experience is recorded in the files covering that type of emergency, to be brought out again for the next similar dispute. The Home Defence system, the government's last-ditch defence against war and internal insurrection, has been found particularly useful in strikes like that of the fire brigades in 1977. On that occasion the county level of the Home Defence network was activated in many areas, with county control rooms being used as the strike-breaking headquarters where the military and civilian emergency services controllers could operate in tandem (see chapter six for details).

Jeffery and Hennessy say on this issue:

'In any emergency there is a fall-back in the home defence system, which comprises regional seats of government, designed to co-ordinate administration after a nuclear attack. If there is a severe breakdown of food distribution arising from an industrial dispute, the home defence emergency feeding depots, using strategic stockpiles of food, might be activated as a last resort. Short of such desperate circumstances, home defence's secure telephone and telexes are a useful adjunct to the often overloaded lines between the Regional Emergency Committees and London.'[28]

These Regional Emergency Committees (RECs) form a second emergency regional structure which can be utilised either in conjunction with, or as an alternative to, the use of troops. The CCU can activate the REC network to monitor local crisis points, mitigate the effects of the dispute through liaising with trade unions, and, if a state of emergency has been declared, exercise executive functions.

The key officials on the RECs are believed to meet regularly in another capacity, as Regional Economic Planning Boards, but on instructions from the CCU, the board chairpersons (normally Regional Directors of the Department of the Environment) summon their equivalents from the other government departments, plus representatives of the local authorities, police and military, to form the RECs.[29] This arrangement was seen working most publicly during the 1979 lorry drivers strike (see pages 140-1) when 11 RECs were set up. The CCU and RECs together established a very smooth-running system for keeping supplies moving and communicating with trade union officials. National strikes in other industries would see similar networks set up, as the key to breaking widespread strikes has proved in the past to be the ability to devolve co-ordinating, administrative and intelligence gathering functions.

The Armed Forces

The troops used in strike-breaking are the ordinary personnel of the armed forces; there is no one specially trained force specifically allocated to MACM. Troops are normally drawn from those units available in Britain with personnel serving in Northern Ireland or the British Army of the Rhine being left on those deployments as long as possible.

However, some troops are more likely than others to find themselves on MACM duties. The armed forces are almost a complete society of their own, with personnel trained in nearly all civilian industrial skills and, when a particular strike-breaking talent is required, the military turn first to its troops specialising in that area. The Ministry of Defence says that no MACM instruction is given in the basic training for ordinary members of the armed forces ('The army does not carry out any training specifically to fit soldiers for use in an industrial dispute.'[30]) But, as John Gilbert, MoD Minister of State said in 1977: 'The nature of service training is such as to provide a number of service men with useful skills of more general application.'[31] This means, in practice, that, when a dispute is likely to require MACM, troops with service experience in that skill are selected for duty and given further specialist training.

The versatility of military training is shown by the example of the Royal Navy's HMS *Phoenix* Nuclear, Biological, Chemical and Damage Training School at Portsmouth. According to the Navy's own publicity: 'The training [at *Phoenix*] is applicable to naval operations both in war and peace and can be modified to provide assistance in the event of national emergencies such as the firemens strike.'[32]

Ordinary soldiers may not receive specific MACM training until required, but their officers have to study the structure of British society and its conflicts — including strikes (or, as the Royal College of Defence Studies syllabus for 1976 put it: 'the industrial and social issues that affect Britain's strength and standing in the world.'). At the Staff College at Camberley, the army's training school for tomorrow's generals, officers were shown in a BBC TV series being instructed in counter-insurgency warfare and internal security techniques; one of the subversive groups they were practising suppression of was British trade unionists. Michael Cockerell, writing in the BBC magazine *The Listener,* said: 'The students are convinced that the British way of life is threatened from within. "We are really talking about subversion in industry and in the media", the brightest and most thrusting of students told me. "I don't consider myself to be right or even left-wing, but I am quite clear that a number of strikes are politically motivated". Another of the officers said: "The biggest threat we reckon to our sort of society is the communist one and if we think that threat only comprises a great number of tanks sitting on the other side of the Iron Curtain, then we're deluding ourselves".'[33] The Staff College at that time was commanded by General Sir Frank Kitson, the army's most well-known theorist on the use of military force for internal security.

The military skills available for strike-breaking are wide ranging: Royal Navy engine specialists, earmarked for running power stations; thousands of HGV licence holders (mainly army), able to drive civilian lorries; army Royal Engineers who can operate water and sewage pumping stations; oil (including petrol) handling training through the army petroleum depot in Dorset; warders for military prisons, used during the 1980 prison officials dispute; fire-fighting training via the RAF and RN specialist establishments (fire is a serious risk to ships and airfields): railway and docks operation through the Royal Corps of Transport; plus all the other military personnel working in the armed forces: postal services, catering, medicine, computers, electronics, etc.

Not all civilian occupations are susceptible to military takeover, however. The Ministry of Defence can only supply a labour force of just over 20,000 at any one time without endangering its purely military commitments, which may be enough to take over a national, non-labour intensive industry (such as the fire service) or a localised labour intensive one (the London Docks in the 1940s), but is inadequate for a national, labour intensive service such as the coal miners.

Increasingly, however, the military's abiity to intervene in strikes is dependent not so much on the amount of labour available but on the level of skill the troops possess. With the mechanisation and automation of formally manual jobs like dockwork and power stations operation the demands for sheer numbers of troops has gone down while the technical ability required has risen dramatically. Increasingly MACM is needing specialists, whether to drive large lorries, run container terminals or operate power stations.

Military intervention in strikes is very much a male affair. The British armed forces generally have always been very male-oriented, and until very recently women only carried out menial tasks or traditionally female work such as secretaries and nurses. Since the late 1970s women have been allowed to move into more skilled, formerly male areas, most notably in communications, but with the main aim of releasing men for the 'real' work of the services: actual combat. The military apparently class interventions in strikes as combat, for women are only very rarely, if ever, seen at the point where troops meet strikers. Only in the biggest military strike deployments, such as the 1977 fire brigade strike, are women visible in any numbers and then just in base-area support work, releasing men for more 'front-line' duties.

As the civilian work has become more complex, the military have also come to rely more heavily on the managerial and supervisory staff in an industry remaining at work to instruct the new workforce in its task. Military success in breaking strikes in power stations, water and sewage pumping plants, the fire service and similar industries now depends on the willingness of the striking workers' supervisors (themselves often trade unionists) to stay at their posts and co-operate with the military.

In the busiest period of military strike-breaking in modern times, 1945-50, the Labour government had available a huge services workforce containing tens of thousands of both unskilled and skilled troops capable of running almost any of the country's essential industries. But the situation is different now. Frank Kitson (see above) talks in his book *Low Intensity Operations* of the 'need to keep enough specialist individuals and units within the army to enable essential civil services to be maintained in the event of civilians being unable or unwilling to maintain them. . . . As the army has contracted (since the end of the Second World War), many of these capabilities have been sacrificed in order that remaining resources can be concentrated in the most important areas. . . but it is necessary to suggest that the greatest care should be taken before any more cuts are made in this direction.'[34]

The then Conservative Minister of State for Defence, Lord Balniel, was specifically questioned about this section of Kitson's book by the Labour opposition in June 1972. Would the government 'disown and dissociate' themselves from it, Roy Hattersley MP asked in the House of Commons.[35] Balniel replied that he had begun reading the book a few days before but had not then reached that page! He did state, however, that the book 'is regarded as being of valuable assistance to troops'.

Essential Industries

The contingency planners are, however, currently preparing to break strikes only in a limited range of industries: those affecting essential services and supplies.

Top of the planners' list is energy supplies, particularly electricity, gas and oil. Other key sectors are the water and sewerage services, food (although now not nearly so likely to be affected, as it was in the days of rationing and centralised distribution in the years immediately after the Second World War), shipping and docks, communications, transport, civilian-run sections of the military and the health and emergency services.

Most of the key industries are in the public sector (the most notable exception is oil) and a potential strategy of the 1979

Conservative government's for handling strikes in this area was revealed by a Conservative Party document leaked to the press in May 1978. This report, from the Party's policy group on the nationalised industries, classified those industries into three categories of vulnerability to strikes with: '(a) sewerage, water, electricity, gas and the health service in the most vulnerable group; (b) railways, docks, coal and dustmen in an intermediate group; and (c) other public transport, education, the postal service and telephones, air transport and steel in the least vulnerable group.'[37]

The report rejected proposals to make strikes illegal and any idea of having a strike-breaking corps of volunteers to run mines, trains or power stations. In strikes in industries which 'have the nation by the jugular vein', it argued 'the only feasible option is to pay up.'[38] This policy of giving in to the most powerful workers seems to have been followed by the Conservatives for at least the first three years of their 1979 administration.

The group also put forward proposals to fragment state industries, set them inflexible financial targets and form a large mobile squad of anti-picket police.

Labour Industry Secretary Eric Varley commented that 'the Tories seem determined to put the clock back in ways which would make Mr Heath's damaging battles with the unions look like a vicarage tea party.'[39]

The most essential services of all in a time of economic crisis are, of course, the police and the armed forces. No modern government can forget the way Lloyd George's administration was shaken by the strikes in both the police and the services in 1918 and 1919. As the current economic recession began to bite in the late 1970s, first the Labour government and then their Conservative successors made what appears to have been a successful attempt to buy the allegiance of the forces of law and order, by giving the police and military substantial pay rises, and increasing their status, for example by providing them with more modern equipment. Both the armed forces and the police are forbidden by law to strike.

The Territorial Army and Civilian Volunteers

There are however, two other potential labour forces besides the regular armed services over which governments periodically cast a covetous eye: the Territorial Army and civilian volunteers.

The 70,000-strong TA, now an efficient, modernised standby army trained in internal security techniques, has been ruled out by both civilian and military contingency planners for strike-breaking because it is considered too unreliable for operations against the civilian population.

With their loyalties divided between their civilian and military commitments the TA could not be depended on to obey orders like regular troops when it came to moves against fellow workers. If they were ever mobilised in an extreme emergency it would probably be first to replace regular troops on back-up work so that the regulars could take part in direct operations. Only when all else had failed would the TA be used against British civilians.

Civilian volunteers, on the other hand, could be more reliable than the TA as they come forward by choice. Their potential effectiveness was seen during the 1926 General Strike (see pages 44-6) the last occasion on which they were called upon in large numbers to help break a strike. The major drawbacks with volunteers, besides being untrained, undisciplined and often unfit, are that they would lack the high level of skill the modern strike-breaker needs, and that their appearance on the scene during a dispute is likely to provoke an even more intensely hostile reaction from the strikers than the arrival of the military. Towards the end of the 1979 ambulance crew strikes (see pages 143-4) for example, the police and army had to take over ambulance duties when strike action was briefly intensified following Health Minister David Ennals' call for volunteers to help in hospitals affected by the National Union of Public Employees action.

In the recent past, detailed plans have been made for the use of civilian volunteers in strikes. The 1945-51 Labour government sent all Ministry of Labour offices a circular late in 1948 telling them how to recruit civilian volunteers. It read: 'If an industrial dispute . . . gravely affected the life of the community, the government may decide that the maximum resources of the State shall be used to restore the services suspended by the dispute.' Troops would be used first, but 'In the last resort the government may appeal to all sections of the community to volunteer to undertake work to maintain essential services.' The local Ministry of Labour offices were to be responsible for recruiting and were to put the plan into operation on the receipt of the single code word 'Volunteer'. The first step would be to put up posters saying: 'Ministry of Labour and National Service: Volunteers required urgently for essential services to maintain the life of the nation. Apply at any Employment Exchange.' In 1949 the scheme was modified so that the essential services could themselves approach potential volunteers with the necessary skills.[40]

Margaret Thatcher and some of her ministers in the 1979 Conservative government were keen to use both the TA and civilian volunteers in strikes despite the advice of their contingency planners. In early 1980, according to *The Times,* ministers instructed the CCU to assess the feasibility of using civilian volunteers in essential industries during a future 'Winter of Discontent'. The planners were against the use of civilians but the ministers were keen to pursue the idea because of the difficulties they had encountered during the previous winter.[41] In November 1980, *The Times* said that the 'fierce dispute among ministers about whether it is desirable or practical' to use volunteers was still unresolved.[42] The Home Secretary, William Whitelaw, was said to be the leader of the 'doves', while ranged against them were Michael Heseltine, John Biffen and John Nott. Two weeks earlier the CCU had met in its purely ministerial form in an unsuccessful attempt to settle the argument. Discussion over the summer with local authorities had shown them to be 'cool' on the idea, however and the 'doves' were said to have scored one notable victory by burying the idea that the TA should be used alongside regular troops in strike-breaking. The Defence Secretary, Francis Pym, had persuaded the Prime Minister 'with considerable difficulty' to drop her plans, and also not to use TA drill halls for mustering civilian volunteers.[43]

Currently government policy is to encourage private employers to take on their own volunteers when needed, and to persuade public bodies to liaise with a wide range of volunteer emergency organisations for general emergency assistance that could also be used to provide behind-the-scenes administrative aid in serious strikes (the Civil Aid Group is the most prominent of these). This is where the determined TA soldier may find an opening; as junior Defence Minister Philip Goodhart said: 'It would, of course, be open to any member of the Territorial Army, as a private citizen and out of uniform, individually to volunteer assistance to the appropriate authorities during an emergency just like any member of the public.'[44]

Who Pays?

Military strike-breaking is an expensive business and someone has to pay for it. MoD policy is to send the sponsoring government department the bill for mobilising troops, aiming to recover its extra costs (petrol, stores purchased, etc) but not the basic pay of troops. If the bill comes to less than £10,000 the MoD does not bother to charge, but this is very rare. It is nearly always more than £10,000 and the sponsor department usually (but not always) passes this on to the employing organisation. The main exception to this charging policy is where preparations have been made but troops in the end have not been deployed. Just how much individual strike-breaking operations have cost is not known, but the mobilisation against the 1977 fire brigades strike — the biggest deployment of recent years — must have cost hundreds of thousands, if not millions, of pounds.

In the end, of course, it is the tax and ratepayer who nearly always pays the bill, whether directly for an invoice rendered by the MoD to another public body, or, if the MoD is not charging the recipient for its services, indirectly in funding the maintenance of the armed forces.

References

1. Ministry of Defence, letter to the author, 14 May 1982.
2. A.V. Dicey, *Law of the Constitution* (1959), p.424.
3. S.A. de Smith, *Constitutional and Administrative Law* (1977), p.295.
4. *Chandler* v. *Director of Public Prosecutions* (1964) AC 763.
5. John Burke, *Jowitt's Dictionary of English Law* (1978).
6. *Halsbury's Laws of England*, Vol.8, p.583.
7. *Hansard,* 11 April 1934, col.352.
8. O. Hood Phillips, *Constitutional and Administrative Law* (1973), p.230.
9. L. Radzinowicz, *A History of English Criminal Law* Vol.4 (1968) pp.129-32 and pp.141-52.
10. *The Queen's Regulations for the Army.* Amendment 87 (September 1973) to para J1163 of 1955 edition; subsequently incorporated in the 1975 edition.
11. Robert Mark, *Policing a Perplexed Society* (1977), p.30.
12. *Hansard,* 14 February 1980, Written Answers, col.761.
13. Emergency Powers Act 1964, s.2.
14. See *Halsbury's Laws of England,* Vol.8, paras. 889-891.
15. Hood Phillips, *op. cit.,* p.232.
16. *The Queen's Regulations for the Army,* 1955 edition, para J1165, section XIII, as amended and 1975 edition, para J11.994, chapter 11.
17. *State Research Bulletin,* number 4 (February 1978).
18. *Hansard,* 10 July 1981, Written Answers col.491.
19. *Hansard,* 20 February 1964, cols. 1409-45.
20. *Ibid.,* col.1422.
21. *Ibid.,* col.1444.
22. *Ibid.,* col.1413.
23. *Ibid.,* col.1414.
24. *Ibid.,* col.1445.
25. Keith Jeffery and Peter Hennessy, *States of Emergency* (1983), p.238.
26. Interview with the author, 9 December 1982.
27. Jeffery and Hennessy, *op. cit.,* p.237.
28. *Ibid.,* p.244.
29. *The Times,* 14 November 1979.
30. Under-Secretary of State for the Army, Geoffrey Johnson-Smith MP, *Hansard,* 22 June 1972, col.699.
31. *Hansard,* 6 December 1977, col.1099.
32. From a publicity stand at Portsmouth Dockyard, Navy Day, 28 August 1978.
33. *The Listener,* 10 January 1980. *War School* was broadcast in four parts between 9 and 30 January 1980.
34. Frank Kitson, *Low Intensity Operations* (1971), p.187.

35. *Hansard,* 22 June 1972, col.701.
36. *Ibid.,* col.703.
37. *The Economist,* 27 May 1978.
38. *Ibid.*
39. *Sunday Times,* 28 May 1978.
40. CAB 134/178, EC (0) (50) 3, 13 February 1950.
41. *The Times,* 17 and 18 July 1980.
42. *The Times,* 19 November 1980.
43. *Ibid.*
44. *Hansard*, 10 February 1981, Written Answers col.312.

Part II
SURVEY OF MILITARY INTERVENTION IN INDUSTRIAL DISPUTES

Three

1945-1970

Thursday 26 July 1945 was a landmark in British politics. On that day the people of Britain rejected the Churchill government and voted into office a Labour Party committed to radical reform of pre-war injustices. 'Let us go forward as comrades in a great cause', the new Prime Minister, Clement Attlee, told thousands of cheering Labour supporters at a victory rally in Westminster Central Hall the same evening.

That July day was less of a turning point in the history of contingency planning in Britain. Two days before, the government's contingency planners and Churchill had ordered 600 troops to stand by to unload strike-bound ships at the Surrey Docks in London. Five days after the election, Attlee sent them in to handle the vessels.

The 1945 Labour government took over a country in debt to the Americans and short of most of the essentials of life, particularly food. There was widespread industrial unrest throughout its six years of office, particularly in the vitally important docks through which nearly all the crucial imports came. With the economy balanced on a knife-edge, the government decided, on at least 14 occasions between July 1945 and October 1951, to intervene in these disputes to keep essential supplies moving by drawing on its huge reserve of labour, the armed forces, then swollen to nearly five million through conscription. Churchill is reported to have said, on hearing the 1945 election results: 'I do not feel down at all; I'm not certain the Conservative Party could have dealt with the labour troubles that are coming.'[1]

Some three years later, Lord Montgomery of Alamein, then Chief of the Imperial General Staff, told a close friend that 'he thought the situation [with strikes] . . . was so bleak he might actually be called upon to "take steps"'! "If the thing goes sky high I may have to play a part: and would do so".'[2] Montgomery was not in sympathy with his Labour political masters, describing the Minister of Defence, A.V. Alexander, as 'utterly and completely useless'.[3]

In retrospect, it is clear that Montgomery was over-dramatising the position. His alarm was caused by the level of unofficial union action that took place between 1945 and 1951. Official strikes were effectively ruled out by the support of most union leaders for the Labour government and by the government's powers to declare strikes illegal under Part Two of the Conditions of Employment and National Arbitration Order 1940. Although widely seen as difficult to operate it remained in force until 1951, much criticised by some trade unionists for effectively giving leaders an excuse for not following through the grievances of their rank and file members.

The *Manchester Guardian* summarised, in June 1950, the change that had taken place in the handing of disputes: 'There used to be a healthy distaste for the use of troops in strikes. Nowadays the Ministry of Labour seems almost an appendage to the service departments, and whenever it has an awkward dispute on its hands the army is called in as a matter of course. "Join the army and see Smithfield" is a current Cockney witticism . . . It is a scathing commentary on the Labour government's handling of labour problems that it should rely continually on the services.'[4]

The *Daily Worker* said: 'What strike around wages can be official nowadays? . . . The Minister of Labour has power under the National Arbitration Order to declare that a wage dispute must be submitted to arbitration and that an official strike to enforce a wage claim is likely to be described by him as illegal . . . So a stage has been reached where official strikes are declared illegal and unofficial strikes are met by calling on the troops to do the men's work.'[5]

Public acceptance of military intervention was greatly eased for a few years after the war by the common feeling that the army was almost a 'citizens army' because such a large proportion of the population either had served, or were serving in it. The rationing, discipline and self-sacrifice that most of the British people had endured during the war also prepared them for the economic and social rigours that were to follow. As Jeffery and Hennessy say: 'From the government's point of view, the condition of the people was a policy-makers' boon'.[6]

Contingency Planning, 1945-51

The civil service began planning before the Second World War was over for confrontations with strikers. It did so on its own initiative.[7] On 4 June 1945, Sir Alexander Maxwell, Permanent Under-Secretary at the Home Office, wrote to other Whitehall heads of departments suggesting that the Supply and Transport Organisation should be revived. A subsequent meeting at the Home

Office on 19 June, involving representatives from 18 departments, agreed on the need for future emergency planning and Maxwell subsequently drew up a memorandum summarising the conclusions for presentation to the next government.

James Chuter Ede, Labour's new Home Secretary, was shown the memorandum very soon after the election and on 22 August he wrote to Attlee recommending that the Cabinet should discuss resuscitating the STO. 'Nothing in Ede's note suggested that he thought the matter was anything more than routine. Indeed, the letter carried no secrecy marking. But it was political dynamite. Here was the first ever majority Labour government, engaged upon the priority task of repealing the Trade Disputes and Trade Unions Act — the embodiment of Baldwin's victory over trade union power [in the General Strike] — being asked by its Home Secretary to consider the reactivation of the sharpest weapon Baldwin had possessed in 1926.'[8]

Attlee, however appreciated the unusual sensitivity of the matter and instead of putting it before the whole Cabinet had a private discussion with his three closest colleagues in the Cabinet on 8 October. The quartet approved the outline of Maxwell's plan and Ede was instructed to carry out a review of emergency planning. The process was given an edge by the dock strike that had just started (see the chronology of strikes that follows).

Before Ede convened his ministerial committee, however, he asked Maxwell to examine certain questions with an inter-departmental committee of officials. Ede circulated this committee's conclusions and his own recommendations in January 1946, recommending that the STO should be re-established, with a ministerial committee making the policy decisions and administration handled by officials and sub-committees.

So far, the civil service-inspired moves to revive the emergencies organisation had progressed surprisingly smoothly, given the ideology of the politicians who were, in theory, in charge of their activities. But this progress was rudely interrupted when Ede's committee met on 29 January 1946. Aneurin Bevan and Sir Stafford Cripps, both on the left of the Labour Party, attacked the plans, saying that apart from other reservations, the move was badly timed: six days earlier the Bill to repeal the Trade Disputes and Trades Unions Act 1927 had been presented to parliament. The committee decided to wait until the Bill had passed through parliament. Bevan and Cripps's more general criticisms of emergency planning were over-ruled by a Cabinet meeting on 8 March when a general policy decision was made to continue with the planning, but in the greatest secrecy.

Once the Bill repealing the 1927 Act had passed its third reading in the House of Lords, the way was clear for contingency planning to resume. On 17 May 1946, another Home Office conference for departmental representatives was held, this time chaired by the man who had succeeded Alexander Maxwell, Sir Frank Newsam. The conference appointed Newsam the convenor of a co-ordinating committee, with seven sub-committees, with the task of preparing detailed emergency plans. Newsam was to remain in charge of the emergencies organisation until 1957.

Newsam's team worked through the remainder of 1946 but the whole operation was surrounded with such secrecy that insufficient contact could be made with outside organisations to make an effective anti-strike apparatus when it was needed. That time came in January 1947, when the road haulage drivers went on strike (see chronology). The government's lack of preparedness for this dispute did focus the Cabinet's attention on emergency planning, however. An Industrial Emergencies Committee had been appointed in October 1945, but did not meet until Attlee was reminded of its existence during the chaos of the road haulage strike; it was then convened, on 15 January 1947, and operated throughout the rest of the dispute.

After the strike, the Cabinet gave the Industrial Emergencies Committee the formal role of co-ordinating government action in strikes and, in April 1947, it was established as a permanent committee under the name of the Emergencies Committee, backed up by a committee of officials, the Emergencies Co-ordinating Committee (renamed the Official Committee on Emergencies in January 1950). This system has remained in existence permanently since then, although under different names.

From the time of the formation of the Emergencies Committee until the June 1948 dock strike there was comparative industrial peace and contingency planning continued steadily, further fleshing out the bones of the system. The many government departments involved in this found that their planning could not proceed beyond an elementary stage without involving industry and local authorities and, although this eroded the secrecy surrounding the process, permission was given in late 1947 for outside contacts to be made. The plans were, thereafter, further developed, particularly during the last year of Attlee's administration, until he lost the October 1950 general election to the Conservatives.

'Churchill's incoming Cabinet, unlike Attlee's, did not discuss the need for an emergencies organisation; its existence was accepted without question. Emergency planning, had finally become part of the "seamless robe" of modern British administration. By the end of 1951, the broad outline of the contemporary emergency machine had become well established. To a very great extent it was a straightforward revival of the pre-war arrangements.'[9]

1945: First Dock Strike

Troops intervened in civilian industrial disputes at least 14 times between 1945 and 1951, with at least two interventions in each year. Seven disputes were in the docks and a further three also involved the transportation or handling of essential supplies. Of the remaining four, two were by energy workers, one by the operators of Tower Bridge and the last was at Buckingham Palace, where the Royal Family was without hot water.

The new Labour government inherited a 10-week-old industrial dispute in the docks that had already seen military involvement. Dockworkers in London, Glasgow, Grimsby, Immingham, Cardiff and Swansea had been taking various forms of industrial action since early May to try to bring their pay rates up to near the industrial average and to improve their general conditions.

When 4,500 dockers came out on strike in Glasgow around Wednesday 11 May, troops were called in within three days to discharge perishable cargoes. Port workers at Grimsby and Immingham on the Humber were striking at the same time and, at the end of the week, troops were unloading a Danish ship at Grimsby with eggs and butter on board and two supply ships at Immingham.[10] These disputes were quickly settled with the port authorities but, when the strike at Swansea entered its second week without a settlement in sight, troops were also used there to unload cargoes.[11] The next port to see use of the military was Cardiff, when the troops started work on 22 July.

During this time a go-slow had been operating in the London docks. Attempts by the Transport and General Workers Union officials and the government to persuade the dockers to go back to work failed and, on 25 July, the day before the general election results were announced, 600 soldiers were brought from the north of England to stand by at the worst hit area, the Surrey Commercial Docks. The six days they waited there saw a change of government, and the dockers at Swansea and Cardiff return to work. On 31 July, 3-400 of the troops started unloading seven of the dozen affected ships, including some carrying timber. The presence of troops led to an immediate walk-out by tally clerks and lightermen in the dock and the troops then had to try to handle these jobs as well. Seven soldiers were reported to have been injured in one morning.[12]

When the military intervention failed to force the dockers back to work, the employers took disciplinary action and withheld attendance money from some employees. Legal action by the dockers to retrieve this money failed and this defeat, on top of all their other setbacks, led the men to call off the go-slow on 13 August and seek further support from other trade unions.

1945: Second Dock Strike

The autumn dock strike of 1945 was much more extensive than that in the summer, involving 43,000 strikers and 21,000 strike-breaking troops at its height. The unofficial strike was an angry rank and file protest against wage rates, working conditions and what many saw as the corrupt and undemocratic nature of the main union involved, the TGWU. Grievances against the TGWU hierarchy were a common thread running through the early post-war dock strikes.

What was to become a national stoppage began at Birkenhead on 25 September and spread rapidly until 30,000 dockers were out at numerous ports by 9 October. The same day, the government announced that troops were going to be used to unload essential cargoes. 'Less than three months after taking office for the first time with an overall majority, a Labour government contemplated the use of troops to break a strike, apparently without any dissent from the ministers around the Cabinet table.'[13]

The strike spread further, the TGWU officials alleging, on 12 October, that left-wing elements were manipulating the strike. The strike leaders vigorously denied this and, with 39,000 dockers on strike and 16,000 troops at work on 16 October, they began moves to start what looked like a new union. This sent the union leaders back to the negotiating table but the failure of these talks to produce more than a reorganisation scheme for the industry led to more dockers joining the strike.

A delegate conference of all the unions involved on 23 October called on the strikers to go back while further negotiations took place, a plan which met with a mixed response. On 30 October, the Government said that the situation had become so serious that troops were going to be used to unload all cargoes, not just those which were immediately essential. By 1 November, 43,000 striking dockers had been replaced by 21,000 troops, some of them Royal Engineer specialists who had worked on the Mulberry Harbours after D-Day.[14]

At this point, however, the strikers decided they could probably gain no more and they voted to go back to work, as the conference had suggested. Work was resumed on 5 November. At the end of the month an official committee was set up to look into the docker's grievances. Its report, on 11 November, recommended a 3*s*. increase on the 16*s*. daily basic rate, a third of the amount the dockers had originally asked for. At the same time the Dock Workers (Regulation of Employment) Act was passed, in part to deal with some of their other complaints.

In this, as in most of the 1945-51 strikes, although the strikers strongly opposed the use of troops, they were not, actively hostile to the service personnel as individuals. Jack Dash, the former leader of the dockers and member of the unofficial Port Workers' Defence Committee, later recalled the commonly-held feelings: 'There was no real anger against the troops themselves. It was only one year after most of the dockers had been troops themselves. Our only anger was against the Labour government; this was the last thing we expected. They were no real threat to the dockers, as they were unskilled. I don't know if any were killed, but quite a few were maimed. A couple of dockers' sons were up on a charge because they refused to do the work. None of the troops wanted to do it — there was no jingoism amongst them, like there would be today, because they were conscripts. Nowadays, they're all professionals.'[15]

1946: Smithfield and Southampton

Troops intervened in two very brief strikes affecting food supplies in 1946, at Smithfield meat market and Southampton Docks.

A nine-day unofficial strike of warehouse staff at Smithfield market began on 9 April. Three days later, the government hinted that it might use troops and, when a negotiating meeting on 14 April proved fruitless, soldiers were sent in the following day. This prompted an immediate walk-out by 3,000 meat porters and the government then withdrew the troops so that they would go back to work. The strike ended on 16 April after an appeal by TGWU General Secretary, Arthur Deakin.

Southampton Docks were brought to a standstill on 6 July when 2,000 dockers came out on unofficial strike after the port authorities had tried to cut manning levels. The TGWU told the strikers to go back to work but they refused. Troops were sent in on 8 July, with the first detachment of 40 soldiers loading meat for the Channel Islands, followed by others unloading fruit and vegetable cargoes. The arrival of the troops prompted an immediate walk-out by crane drivers but the strike ended on 11 July before it became more serious.

Just before the armed forces were mobilised in February 1947 to help in the chaos caused by the severe winter weather, Operation Eatables was mounted in London to break a major strike by road transport workers. The unofficial strike, over working hours and pay, started in London and quickly spread to other areas, although throughout its duration its worst effects were felt in London.

By 9 January there were nearly 15,000 workers idle and, with the London meat ration threatened, the government announced that emergency measures were to be taken. The following day, a Friday, it was announced that troops from all three armed services would be brought in that Monday to handle meat at Smithfield market.

A government statement said: 'The Ministry of Food was not intervening in the industrial dispute nor implying any opinion on the men's claim.'[16] The military saw their role differently, however: 'Operation Eatables . . . played a vital part in bringing the Transport Strike in London to an end', according to *Army Quarterly*.[17]

The government's announcement on the use of troops prompted further walk-outs and at a meeting of the strikers at Stratford Town Hall that Sunday, they resolved to stay on strike. Other workers at Smithfield and Billingsgate decided to strike in sympathy as soon as troops appeared in their markets. Meanwhile, troops were arriving in London to prepare for the start of 'Eatables'. Clapham Common was turned into a military camp, with prisoners of war helping to erect kitchens, wash-houses and marquees. Beneath the Common, 130 feet down, the Clapham South Deep Tube Shelter, built during the war and capable of housing 3,000 people,[18] became the sleeping quarters for 1,400 troops and the command post for the strike-breaking operation. Officers also carried out a preliminary reconnaissance of the markets.[19]

On the morning of Monday 13 January nearly 3,500 troops, mainly from the Coldstream Guards, moved into Smithfield in 600 lorries, and 2,300 porters came out on strike at once, saying in a statement that they would not go back until the troops were removed. The next day, the initial military force was augmented by 250 naval lorries, followed by 500 from the RAF the following day.

Although there appeared to be little personal ill-feeling between strikers and troops, the principle of military intervention in industrial disputes aroused great resentment and, by 15 January porters at Covent Garden and Borough fruit and vegetable markets, 2,000 dockers and an equal number of Thames lighter handlers went on strike until the troops were withdrawn. The strikers also drew a clear distinction between what they considered essential and non-essential supplies, and they stopped troops loading civilian lorries with non-essentials.[20] By 15 January there were 20,000 transport workers on strike and a special conference voted to stay out. 15 January was also the day that the Cabinet's Industrial Emergencies Committee met for the first time. The government and its contingency planners had been caught unawares by the strike and the IEC was hastily convened to try to retrieve the situation (see page 86 above).

The strike was quickly settled, however, with normal work resuming on 18 January after the Road Haulage Association agreed to further talks, on the understanding that the workers would get a substantial part of their claim.

Army Quarterly thought that overall the strike had been a 'sad and drab affair' but from a military point of view the operation had been a 'first-class show', which had not received 'the attention it deserved'. Moreover, the journal continued: 'Operation Eatables provided an interesting and valuable example of the great value, in these days of trade union indiscipline, in having a disciplined and loyal force able to replace at short notice any section of workers who may see fit to try to hold the community to ransom.'[21]

1947: Dock Strike

Troops were again used in the docks in April 1947. Glasgow dockers had come out on strike late in March in protest against redundancy proposals. After two weeks, 3,800 men were idle and 60 ships tied up. Six dockers delegates travelled round the country explaining their actions to other dockers.

Troops moved into the Glasgow docks on 10 April to unload the *Gracia* carrying food from Canada. The same day the Port Workers Defence Committee in London said that other dockers should support the Glasgow strikers, while the TGWU issued an appeal to its members not to take any unofficial action.

The strike was confined to Glasgow until 28 April when London members of the National Amalgamated Stevedores and Dockers Union, a rival to the TGWU, came out in sympathy with their colleagues in Scotland. On 1 May, with 700 troops at work in Glasgow, the Emergencies Committee made preparations for sending troops into the London docks, where over half of the 125 ships in port were at a standstill. But the military were not needed as the following day the London strikers went back to work, followed two days later by the men in Glasgow.

1947: Tower Bridge

Tower Bridge was closed to road traffic at the end of April 1947 when over 1,000 employees of the City of London Corporation came out on unofficial strike over the promotion of an unpopular police constable at Billingsgate market to sergeant. On Wednesday 30 April, the operators of the steam engines that raised and lowered the bridge ceased work and, as by law the bridge could not be left closed to river traffic, the roadway was raised.

By the end of the week the government claimed that the ensuing traffic chaos was so great that troops were needed to work the bridge. Naval engineers from Chatham were brought in on 3 May and by noon on Monday 5 May had the bridge operating again. This military intervention led to other workers joining the strike, but it was called off on 8 May without the strikers achieving their objective.

1948: Buckingham Palace

The army again mobilised in March 1948 when an industrial dispute left the Royal Family without hot water.

This emergency came about when 1,600 Ministry of Works employees in London, mainly engineer attendants operating lifts and hot water supplies in government buildings, came out on unofficial strike on 15 March over a wage claim.

Buckingham Palace quickly became the symbolic focus of this dispute when, on the second day, soldiers of the Brigade of Guards were sent in to stoke the boilers that provided the Royal Family with hot water. On 17 March, electricians at the Palace meeting in the Royal Mews voted to strike as well if the Guards were not withdrawn within 24 hours, while the following day shop stewards said the strike would be extended on 22 March if the troops were not taken out immediately. The strike was settled in a week, however, when the strikers said they would go back to work and continue negotiations if the troops were withdrawn.

1948: Dock Strike

Another bitter dispute in the docks involving the dockworkers, the government and the TGWU broke out in June 1948 and saw the government declaring the first state of emergency since 1926 and mobilising nearly 2,000 troops.

The unofficial dispute had its origins in the dockworkers continuing dissatisfaction with their pay and conditions and the

TGWU's inability (or refusal) to support action to provide remedies. The strike actually began in Wapping on 12 June following the harsh disciplining of 11 dockers who had protested about the rate they were being paid to unload a 'dirty' cargo of zinc oxide. Within three days, 39 ships and 4,000 workers were idle in what was to become known as the 'Zinc Oxide' strike.

On 16 June a tribunal set up to inquire into the dispute found in favour of the disciplinary action and the TGWU General Secretary Arthur Deakin angered the strikers further by saying that the strike was unjustified. The dispute then escalated rapidly, until, by 22 June, 19,000 of the 27,000 London dockers were on strike. On that day Deakin called a meeting of dockers at the Albert Hall; about 2,000 men turned up and voted to go back. But the unofficial strike leaders had called a meeting at Victoria Park, Hackney, at exactly the same time which attracted about 6,000 strikers, who decided to stay out.

The following day, 17 June, 300 soldiers from the Guards regiments at Wellington Barracks were sent to Poplar, loading civilian lorries with perishable goods then accumulating on the quayside, while the government watched to see how the strike would develop. On Thursday 24 June, with nearly 20,000 dockers and over 150 ships idle the Cabinet ordered 1,000 sailors, 3,000 RAF personnel and 2,000 soldiers to stand by to intervene the following Monday. Over the weekend the services made detailed plans; the Navy, in what it called Operation Zebra, was to provide technically skilled ratings to operate the dock equipment. The Cabinet hoped the strikers would go back to work on the Monday but they did not and 1,600 troops were sent into Poplar docks in the morning to unload food. When the Cabinet met at 11.00 that morning it heard that the strike had then spread to Merseyside.

With no relief in sight, the Cabinet decided to declare a state of emergency that afternoon. Before any emergency powers were utilised, however, Attlee made a radio appeal to the strikers at 9.00pm the same evening. He said: 'The government cannot in any way recognise or deal with those who are leading an unofficial strike . . . This is not a strike against capitalists or employers. It is a strike against your mates; a strike against the housewife; a strike against the ordinary common people . . . Your clear duty to yourselves, to your fellow citizens and to your country is to return to work.'[22]

The declaration of the emergency and Attlee's emotional appeal tipped the scales in the strike and, a mass meeting of the strikers in Victoria Park on 29 June decided to go back to work.

The strike committee's recommendation said: 'In view of the complete line up of reactionary forces against us and considering the complacent attitude of the responsible parties — that is, the employers, the higher trade union officials and the government — we, the strike committee, are recommending all men back to work tomorrow.'[23] *The Times* noted with some disquiet that, although the strike had been broken, the unofficial leaders retained their 'control' over the dockers. The TGWU itself, as in the 1945 strike and those still to come, was seen by them as the enemy.[24]

1949: Dock Strikes

In May 1949, for the fourth time in four years, the dockers clashed with the employers, the government and their union. This time it was not over their own position but in sympathy with their collegues in the Canadian Seamen's Union which the Canadian government and shipowners were trying to suppress. The CSU was on strike and had appealed to British dockers for assistance.

The government's subsequent *Review of the British Docks Strike 1949* found that the stoppages in Britain had occurred in three distinct stages: first, in the Bristol Channel ports and Liverpool, starting on 1 May and ending with an unconditional return to work by 15 June; second, in London from 20 to 23 June; and third, the most important stage, from 26 June to 23 July, involving another state of emergency and the mobilisation of 12,792 troops.[25]

The first stage of the strikes had been rumbling since a Canadian ship was blacked in the London Docks on 3 April. On 14 May the Canadian *Montreal City* arrived in Avonmouth with a blackleg crew and, when the dockers refused to handle the ship, the employers threatened to penalise them and this provoked a lightning strike which then became a form of lock-out. This in turn brought sympathy action by other workers at Avonmouth and Bristol.

The Cabinet, on 23 May, told the Emergency Committee to 'familiarise' itself with the strike and make advance preparations for handling it.[26] Three days later the Committee decided to send troops to Avonmouth immediately to unload food ships. The arrival of troops prompted further sympathy strike action at Avonmouth on 27 May and also at Liverpool when a Canadian ship, originally destined for the Bristol Channel, docked there.[27] The strike then escalated quickly, with 11,000 out in Liverpool and the Bristol Channel by 2 June. But by this time also the government had sent over 1,200 troops from the three services into Avonmouth and Bristol and was confident that they should be able to handle all ships there, not just those with essential cargoes. The

Liverpool strikers eventually went back on 13 June and those in the Bristol Channel on 15 June but the dispute was by no means settled.

The second stage of the dispute was a brief strike by members of the National Amalgamated Stevedores and Dockers Union in London that served more as a portent of what was to come when, on 26 June, the main phase of the strike started.

By the end of June 7,000 dockers and 69 ships were idle, with the workers claiming they had been locked out. On 6 July, with 8,500 dockers and 92 ships affected, the government decided to use troops and sent them in the next day. This provoked more walk-outs and on 8 July the Home Secretary, Chuter Ede, warned that a state of emergency would be declared unless the docks returned to normal within three days. 'The only effect was to ensure that Watermen, Lightermen, Tugmen and Bargemen also joined in.'[28]

The state of emergency was duly declared on 11 July, taking effect from midnight that night. The dispute then escalated. By 14 July there were 14,300 dockers and 134 ships idle, while the number of troops involved had risen to 4,500 from 1,700 five days before. By 18 July the number of dockers involved had risen to 16,340, but with 6,600 troops then working the number of idle ships had dropped to 71. The troop level was to rise to a peak of 12,792 on 23 July.

After the state of emergency was declared the government made emergency regulations which came into force on 12 July. These enabled the Minister of Transport to set up an Emergency Committee to control the Port of London, with a main office in the Ministry building in Berkeley Square and another in dockland. The Emergency Committee, meeting daily, oversaw the working of the Port Committee, set up by the Port of London Authority, which handled the day-to-day running of the docks with representatives of the services present.

One of the aims of the Emergency Committee was to build up the military labour force in the docks 'with the object of restoring the port to full working life.'[29] By 23 July, all ships that could be worked were being handled either by troops (130 ships) or non-striking dockers (13). Troops handled 139,129 tons of cargo in those 11 days. The official *Review* concluded that they had done a 'magnificent job and the rate of output which they achieved gave great satisfaction.'[30]

A mass meeting of the strikers at Victoria Park on 21 July voted to go back to work when the CSU, having obtained certain minor concessions, terminated its dispute as far as Britain was concerned. The government's *Review* of the strike was very disturbed, however, by the lengths to which the ordinary British worker was prepared to go in taking solidarity action with comrades overseas, going directly against the wishes of the TGWU: 'The men owe it to themselves, their families and their fellow trade unionists to give loyal support to their trade union leaders', the Minister of Labour and National Service, G.A. Isaacs, said in the foreword.[31]

1949: London Power Stations

The Cabinet Emergencies Committee faced one of its most difficult problems on 2 December 1949 when it heard that manual workers at four London power stations were planning to start an unofficial strike over a possible loss of pay. The Committee was told, however, that 480 troops could probably effectively replace the strikers and therefore resolved to send them in if the workers struck.[32] The strike started while the next meeting of the Committee was taking place on 12 December and the order was given directly from the meeting.[33]

In fact, only three power stations were affected initially: Enfield, Dartford and Willesden. One thousand workers came out, to be replaced by 131 troops, whose job was to help the non-striking engineers to maintain the services. The use of troops actually provoked the workers at the fourth station, Barking, to come out the next day. This very large plant was closed down at 3.30pm, but by the same evening, personnel from the RAF had been sent in and were trying to restart it. There were power cuts on a large scale in the afternoon.

On 14 December, union officials talked to the strikers in an attempt to settle the dispute, while troops also took over the cranes on the Barking coal wharf. After hearing their leaders the strikers decided to go back the following day.

From the point of view of the Communist paper, the *Daily Worker*: 'the Ministry [of Labour] has the troops in the docks, the meat market or the power stations in the twinkling of an eye. Never was a recalcitrant employer or public authority in dispute with a union so sure of a speedy alternative supply of strike-breakers as they are under the present Labour Minister.' It added: 'The trade union leaders who remain silent in such a situation are acquiescing in a vile, anti-trade union practice which cuts at the very foundations of the movement.'[34]

1950: Dock Strike

The first meeting of the new Official Committee on Emergencies (see page 86) was on 13 April 1950 to discuss the possibility of a dock strike following the expulsion from the TGWU of three of the leaders of the 1949 unofficial stoppage.

The 1950 dock strike was the culmination of five years of conflict between radical rank and file dockers and the TGWU leadership. The union's special committee that recommended the expulsions also declared that the unofficial Port Workers' Defence Committee and its newspaper, the *Port Workers' News,* were subversive bodies and any union member associating with them would be liable to severe disciplinary action. When the three men's appeal against expulsion from the union was rejected on 18 April the PWDC called an immediate meeting in Canning Town, East London. The 3,000 dockers present resolved to strike from the next day, 19 April.

On Thursday 20 April a Cabinet meeting in the morning discussed the situation but decided against the immediate use of troops. The Ministerial Committee on Emergencies met for the first time in 1950 that evening in the Foreign Secretary's room in the House of Commons and, anticipating that the strike was going to spread rapidly, authorised the Home Secretary, Chuter Ede, to request service ministers to make preparations for troops to be available from Monday 24 April. At the next day's Cabinet meeting, Ede reported that 1,000 troops could be available from 24 April and that military officers in 'mufti' (plain clothes) would be visiting the docks on 23 April to plan the work of the troops.

Also on 21 April, with 8,000 dockers on strike along the Thames, the PWDC held another mass meeting. It offered to end the strike if a ballot of all port workers was organised so that every worker could express their opinion about the expulsions.

The TGWU made no satisfactory response to this move and, on 24 April, with the strike intensified to the point where 12,000 dockers were on strike, 1,000 troops were sent into the docks. Arrangements were made by the government to increase this number by 1,000 troops each day until by the end of a fortnight 20,000 would be at work; 'the maximum effort which they could make.'[35]

On 26 April, with 14,400 dockers on strike, the MCE heard that there were then over 3,000 troops at work and agreed to continue building up troop levels; meanwhile bus crews and tug operators considered sympathetic action.

The London Dock Labour Board, however, issued a threat to the strikers on 27 April that if they did not return to work by Monday 1 May they would be expelled from the industry. A major in the Royal Engineers was heard to say on 28 April: 'I hope the bally strike doesn't finish before Monday. We want a chance to perfect our organisation this time, eh?'[36] A mass meeting on 29 April agreed to go back and fight the expulsions through the union branches and the troops were withdrawn from the London area on 2 May.[37]

Two weeks later, the OCE met to review the operation of the contingency plans during the dock strike. It was generally agreed that the arrangements had worked well without using the Emergency Powers Act 1920. It was also felt that, after so many London dock strikes, 'the number of men and types of skill required to work the Port of London were now fairly well-known to the Service Departments but it might be desirable for similar information to be available about other ports.'[38] A major concern of this meeting was the question of accommodation for troops on strike-breaking duties in London. On this occasion tents had been provided in the Royal Parks but in winter this would not be realistic and buildings might have to be requisitioned under the Defence Regulations. The Committee decided to ask the Ministry of Works to carry out a survey of likely buildings in consultation with the military, but it was stressed that 'care should be taken to maintain secrecy about these preparations'[39] (see page 104). This OCE meeting also discussed plans for a gas industry strike (see pages 100-102).

1950: Smithfield and Beyond

A pay dispute at Smithfield market almost led to the first government use of civilian volunteers for strike-breaking since the 1926 General Strike.

Fifteen hundred meat lorry drivers at Smithfield came out on unofficial strike on 24 June in protest at delays in settling their claims for a 19*s.* wage increase. A meeting of the Ministerial Committee on Emergencies at mid-day on 26 June heard that troops could be in action within two days if needed. There was some hesitation about issuing the order, however because, as the Minister of Defence said: 'too frequent use of the Services in industrial disputes not only prejudiced their training but might create ill will against them among the workers.'[40] Arrangements were put in hand to bring in the troops on 28 June and these were implemented when TGWU General Secretary, Arthur Deakin, failed to persuade the strikers to go back to work at a mass meeting in Poplar that same evening. On the morning of 28 April military lorries and crews began distributing canned corned beef from buffer depots (emergency civil defence stores) to retail butchers in London in order to maintain the supply of meat.

As frequently happened, the use of troops led directly to the extension of the dispute; when troops started handling meat on 3 July, Smithfield porters refused to touch it and they in turn were replaced by service personnel. The services move into Smithfield had been preceded by a plain-clothes reconnaisance of the market by officers.[41]

On 4 July the Cabinet, the Ministerial Committee on Emergencies and the Official Committee on Emergencies all met at various times to discuss the deepening crisis. With 640 military vehicles and 2,000-3,000 troops being used, the OCE was told that accommodation was becoming problematic and the Ministry of Works offered to make a Deep Tube Shelter available. The army, represented by an aptly named Colonel Clapham, expressed the view that the 3,000-space Clapham Deep Shelter was their choice and steps were taken to make it ready for use.

The Ministerial Committee was told by the OCE that workers for the wholesale provision merchants had also walked out over the use of troops and it was then agreed to replace them too. Plans were also made to use naval ratings to take over the maintenance of the meat cold stores if needed and to unload ships. The Committee heard that the BBC had asked the Ministry of Food if it might use film of troops working at Smithfield in its TV broadcasts. The nervous Committee thought that this was 'undesirable and that the BBC should be dissuaded.'[42] All this was reported to the Cabinet for approval.

The *Daily Worker* reported on 5 July that: 'All accepted rules and bye-laws were being ignored by the authorities yesterday as they rushed troops to clear the strike-bound Smithfield market of meat. Servicemen, inexperienced in the handling and stacking of meat, bundled as much as possible into the army and RAF trucks and vans, often walking across frozen meat to do so. The trucks yesterday were not insulated as required by law, and the drivers often unknowingly committed offences. As the lorries stood in line, held up by the traffic jams, the drivers ran their engines and so allowed the exhaust fumes to seep through to the frozen carcasses.'[43]

By Thursday 6 July the position had deteriorated to the point where the London meat ration would run out by the end of the week and the Cabinet therefore approved a Home Office plan to use troops in the highly sensitive dock areas to take meat from cold stores from 10 July with the prospect of having to unload ships two to three days later, almost certainly provoking a dockworkers strike.

The road haulage drivers now entered the fray, however, and tipped the scales beyond military control. Incapable of replacing all of the strikers with troops, the contingency planners started to take steps to call for civilian volunteers.

The OCE meeting on 8 July was told that only 1,450 military drivers could be spared for the lorry drivers strike due to start on 10 July. As this was clearly not enough, preliminary preparations were made for the recruitment of volunteers (see page 78 for details of the government's plan for recruiting volunteers).

Before any ministers had a chance to consider this highly emotive method of strike-breaking the dispute ended. On 10 July, the day the strike was to be extended, Deakin persuaded the strikers to go back. The troops were not deployed in the docks and civilian volunteers were never summoned.

1950: Gas Strike

The difficulties involved in handling a strike in the gas industry occupied a considerable amount of the OCE's time in 1950, before and during the strike which finally broke out in London's gas works in October.

The gas industry was particularly problematic for the contingency planners as it was decentralised, with over 1,000 local gas works to be operated and no equivalent of the electricity national grid.

Early in May 1950 the civil servant commanding the OCE, Frank Newsam, prepared a paper for the Committee on *Arrangements for Maintenance of Gas Supplies in an Emergency*.[44]

Newsam said that it was essential at the start of a strike that alternative labour was available at short notice in order to maintain continuity of operations such as retort-firing. 'In the first instance', he believed, 'the alternative labour would have to be supplied by the services.' In a national strike there would not be enough troops actually to run the gas works and civilian volunteers would be needed.

Newsam suggested that, in a widespread (but not general) gas strike, there would have to be a regional control system for the strike breaking operation and he put forward the following proposal: Area Gas Boards should group themselves by the army's administrative/geographical commands and appoint one liaison officer to each representing all the gas boards in the region. The navy and RAF would also appoint liaison officers to the army HQs. No steps to call in troops could be taken without specific ministerial authority, which would be conveyed to the Board through the Ministry of Fuel and Power.

He continued: 'It would normally be for the Official Committee on Emergencies to advise Ministers on this point, to consider any general questions of principle which might be raised, to authorise the total number of servicemen to be used and to give directions as to how they were to be distributed among the army commands. Subject to this, the allocation, dispositions and duties of servicemen would be worked out between the army commands and the Area Gas Boards.'

In this hypothetical widespread, but not general, gas strike the regional organisation of the OCE would not need to be activitated as there would be no competing claims for labour or supplies. In the event of a general gas strike, however, or a gas strike with linked strikes in other industries, the Regional Committees would be brought into action to undertake many of the co-ordinating functions of the OCE.

Newsam's innovating paper was discussed at the OCE meeting on 16 May 1950 and initial plans were made to implement it. The minutes show, however, that the politicians nominally responsible for this policy had not had an opportunity to discuss what was being done in their name before a gas strike broke out.

The unofficial gas strike of September-October 1950 was another bitter fight between the shop-floor on the one hand and the union leaders, employers, government and armed services on the other. It was also the last strike during the governments of 1945-51 to see military intervention.

The strike began in mid-September when union officials agreed a wage rise with the employers that many union members considered too low. By 20 September some 1,500 maintenance workers were on strike from 15 works in the North Thames Gas Board area and three in the Eastern area, although supervisory staff were carrying out much of their work.

The OCE met on 26 September to discuss the situation and consider how feasible it would be to use troops. It concluded that service personnel could, in fact, handle the current dispute although a large number of technicians would be needed. The MCE, meeting the next day for its only discussion on the dispute, agreed with the report from the OCE, and decided not to use troops immediately. This was ratified by the Cabinet meeting on the following day (28 September), which recognised that military involvement could lead to an extension of the strike.

The eventual military intervention in the strike was relatively short-lived, lasting from 5 October until around 9 October, when, with 68 service personnel working at Beckton, Bow and Fulham (although 4,400 were standing by) the strike was called off. An important element in both exacerbating and ending the strike was the government's use of Order 1305, a war-time law making certain forms of industrial action illegal. The Attlee government rediscovered the order and jailed 10 of the strike leaders under it on 5 October, as the troops were moving in.

With the experience of the first gas strike behind them, the OCE officials went back to considering the overall contingency plan for gas strikes which Newsam had drawn up earlier in the year.[45] This had not been submitted to the Ministerial Committee because of the parliamentary summer recess and now, in view of the strike, it was decided to consider it. Electricity supplies were also brought within the remit of the review.

The revised plan[46] considered that the autumn strike had shown that safety in this case had never been in jeopardy, little advance planning had been needed and skilled naval personnel had been capable of carrying out repairs. On the other hand, it was clear that in a general strike the military would not be able to cope, although in localised disputes there was reason to be more optimistic. Because of this, the Committee felt it was 'of the greatest importance' that the army commands should be able to get some idea of the kind of problems that would arise in a strike in their area. It was recommended that senior army staff should be shown 'what type of work is involved in a gas works' and should be given a map showing locations of local gas works and some overall figures as to the numbers of workers employed there.

The Committee also suggested that there should be direct personal liaison between army commands and the 12 Area Gas Boards at the highest level, while stressing that it was 'important to avoid any detailed preparation which might come to the notice of the gas workers.'

This emergency plan for a military takeover of the gas industry had also been drawn up with the electricity industry in mind; as early as August 1950, the military 'already had details of the number of servicemen (including technicians) necessary to operate power stations in London and elsewhere.'[47]

These preparations reflected the OCE's concern over the whole question of energy supplies, vital to the running of an advanced industrial society. The other main fuel after gas and electricity was oil and highly secret plans were also made for military assistance here.

Some contingency plans regarding oil had already been made following the harsh winter and fuel shortages of early 1947 but the OCE meeting on 11 July asked the Ministry of Fuel and Power to obtain unofficially from the oil industry 'data which would enable plans to be made for the maintenance of essential supplies in the event of a strike.'[48] The Ministry discretely approached an emergencies committee set up by the four major oil companies which said that the biggest problem in a strike would arise in London where the labour force was least reliable and that the industry wanted to discuss with the military the 'kind of help which might be given by them in an emergency and how it should be obtained.'[49]

The Ministry of Fuel thought that this should be done at HQ level as it 'might be embarrassing if by some mischance' the existence of the talks became known.[50] The OCE on 5 November 1950 gave the go-ahead for these talks and this was ratified by the MCE on 11 December. Throughout, a principal concern of officials and politicians was that these discussions should remain secret. They must have been aware that their moves could have been seen by employees as a Labour government offering to supply a major private industry with a military, strike-breaking force to undermine the workers' interests. As a senior official in the Ministry of Labour and National Service, Sir Guildaume Myrddin-Evans, said, knowledge of these discussions 'might cause unrest in the industry.'[51] So delicate was the whole issue that the OCE issued a caveat to the industry along with their co-operation: 'The oil companies should be told that [the plans] were secret and precautionary only and did not imply that the government would be prepared to put in servicemen'.[52] In January 1951, the Ministry of Fuel and Power convened a meeting of representatives from the War Office and the oil industry, where both sides agreed to appoint liaison officers and the military made clear what further notice and information it would require.[53] It appears that the plans were then implemented during the 1953 oil tanker drivers strike (see page 105).

1951: Ready and Waiting

During the last few months of its life, the Labour government's contingency planners prepared for military intervention in six industrial disputes; in the event no mobilisations took place.

The February dock strike saw 8,000 workers out on Merseyside followed by dockers in London a few days later. The services were prepared to intervene on the Mersey, but, the War Office expressed great reluctance to do so because of the effect it would have on other military commitments.[54] Intervention plans were made and troops put on standby but the dispute ended before they were called on.

A rail dispute, also in February, saw the government considering declaring a state of emergency but deciding against it because: 'When this had been done during the dock strike of 1949 the government had found themselves somewhat embarrassed, having made Emergency Regulations which, while adding little to their existing powers, created an impression that drastic new measures could be taken'.[55] Military assistance with lorries was discounted because not enough were available, but the Air Ministry was asked to discuss with the General Post Office ways of helping with postal deliveries.

A dock strike in Manchester in May led the OCE to consider diverting a ship with an important cargo to a military port to be unloaded by service labour. Less than a fortnight later, the Committee was discussing whether to bring in military lorries following a strike by 11,000 road haulage drivers.

At the beginning of June, there was yet another problem in the docks with tally clerks in London and Tilbury on strike and the Committee discussed the difficulties of military intervention. Two unassociated disputes at Tilbury in October also led to the Committee discussing the use of troops but again they were not needed.

Two other problems preoccupied the contingency planners in 1951: where to house troops on strike-breaking operations in London and how to persuade the BBC to take a stand more favourable to the government when reporting on important strikes.

Where in the capital could the government house the 27,000 troops that would be needed to break a major dock strike? In March 1951 the Ministry of Works, in response to a request made by the Committee on 16 May 1950 (see page 98), came up with an outline plan that had 5,000 troops in tents in the Royal Parks, another 8,000 in tents on RAF land at Hornchurch, 6,600 in barracks — and the rest without accommodation unless the Deep Shelters or large buildings like Earls Court were used. The military were firmly against tents being used in winter and were also dismissive of the Deep Shelters, following their experiences at Clapham in the 1950 Smithfield strike. The Ministry of Works therefore set off to reconnoitre other buildings and open spaces. In October they produced a report suggesting Arsenal, Tottenham and Chelsea football grounds could take a total of 2,200 troops in tents, while suitable buildings for requisitioning included the Locarno Dance Hall in Streatham, the Brixton roller-skating rink, the Albert Hall, Earls Court and Olympia.[56]

The second problem for the government was the BBC, which persisted in editing government statements on the seriousness of strikes so that the intended message was not always broadcast to the strikers in the way the government wanted. The heads of the Home Office, BBC and GPO met for an informal but secret chat at the House of Commons on Friday 19 January 1951. Frank Newsam from the Home Office asked Sir William Haley of the BBC why these urgent statements had been tampered with.

Haley said he would consider the problem, but: 'He felt bound to point out, however, that in the past alterations to government messages had been necessary so as to make them intelligible to the public.'[57] The Home Office and the BBC did eventually agree, however, that more 'co-operation' was needed when it came to broadcasting on matters that might 'further the national interest', and an informal system of liaison was agreed that allowed the BBC to continue to project itself as independent and objective while at the same time being more sympathetic to the government line.

After the repeated military mobilisations of the 1945-51 Labour government, the following 13 years of Conservative rule saw only three instances of Military Aid to the Civil Ministries: the 1953 oil tanker drivers strike, the 1955 railway strike and the 1960 seamens strike; followed by one intervention during the 1964-70 Labour administration, the 1966 seamens strike. This virtual disappearance of the military from the industrial scene resulted from the relative peace that prevailed in the essential industries as governments managed the economy on Keynesian principles in a climate of political consensus.

1953: Oil Tanker Drivers Strike

The unofficial strike of oil tanker drivers in London in October 1953 gave the Official Committee on Emergencies and the oil industry the chance to try out their unique and very secret arrangement drawn up in 1950-51 (see page 103). The strike had complicated origins in demands for more pay, a call for restrictions on non-union labour, grievances against the union (the TGWU) and the use of outside contractors for oil transportation.

On 22 October there were 3,000 workers on strike and the government hinted troops might be used if they did not go back to work. The next day, union officials failed to persuade the strikers to return to work and that evening 2,000 troops were moved into London. The troops started work on Saturday 24 October and, by the end of the day, 4,000 were delivering fuel around the capital. Another 2,000 troops were drafted in on the Sunday so that by Monday morning most London garages had fuel.

This show of strength by the employers and government had its desired effect and the strikers began to return to work on 25

October. A mass meeting on 26 October voted to go back and resume negotiations.

This was the last occasion on which a complete labour force was replaced by troops until the 1973 Glasgow fire brigade strike (see page 119).

1955: Railway Strike

The first post-war military intervention in an *official* industrial dispute came in 1955 when 60,000 railway footplate workers belonging to the Associated Society of Locomotive Engineers and Firemen went on strike on 29 May for higher wages.

The government indicated its strategy for the strike in a statement issued later that same day. It said that the military would be used to keep essential postal services running, with the RAF providing aircraft and the army making lorries available. However, the government said: 'No servicemen are being employed anywhere on the railways'.[58] By avoiding military involvement in the running of the railways themselves, the government avoided alienating the National Union of Railwaymen, whose members remained at work and kept a skeleton service operating.

On 31 May, the government declared a state of emergency to give itself the power to regulate energy supplies, carry mail and give effect to an emergency insurance scheme for private motorists giving lifts to other people. The strike proved relatively unproblematic however, and negotiations continued for a fortnight, when a settlement was reached.

During the dispute 600 military vehicles and 760 drivers assisted the Post Office, while RAF Transport Command moved nearly a million pounds of mail.

1960 and 1966: Seamens Strikes

The two occasions on which troops intervened in industrial disputes during the 1960s both involved the Royal Navy ferrying essential supplies to Scottish islands cut off during strikes by members of the National Union of Seamen.

Years of dissatisfaction with seamen's Victorian employment conditions, low wages, and the denial of basic workers rights by the Merchant Shipping Acts, plus concern by many members at the apparent close identity between their union and the ship owners, boiled over in the summer of 1960 into a protracted and angry unofficial strike by Merchant Navy crews. The strike was sparked off on 6 July by the disciplining of four men under the Merchant Shipping Act 1894, but quickly developed into a protest at the NUS's delay in obtaining a 44-hour working week. The strike was called off temporarily on 20 July and then resumed on 10 August following the strikers' clarification of their own demands. They were then protesting more precisely about the unrepresentative and, some said, corrupt nature of the NUS and hoped for a massive initial stoppage. When this failed to materialise, the National Seamen's Reform Movement (denounced by NUS General Secretary, Tom Yates, as 'glib-tongued trouble makers'[59]) concentrated on trying to organise a prolonged stoppage, but failed and the strike was called off on 26 September.

Military intervention took place in the first phase of the strike after the Scottish Office announced on 15 July that certain Scottish islands (particularly Coll, Tiree and Barra) were running short of essential supplies. On 17 July Royal Navy boom defence vessels delivered nearly 30 tons of foodstuffs in the Western Isles.[60]

The 1966 NUS strike was the Union's first official strike for over 40 years and was authorised by Union officials partly because of intense rank and file dissatisfaction with pay and conditions and partly to stop this militancy resulting in the formation of a breakaway union that would have destroyed the NUS.

The strike lasted from 16 May until 30 June, by which time 26,000 seamen and 800 ships were affected. The government floated the idea of using the navy to run essential supplies to the Scottish islands on the first day of the strike, at the same time emphasising that it was not immediately thinking of using the armed forces for other roles in the strike.[61]

'Operation Shortbread' began in fact on Wednesday 18 May when three warships (the coastal minesweepers *Belton* and *Wotton* and the boom defence vessel *Laymoor*) sailed from Scottish ports.

On board were bread, milk, paraffin and perishable groceries (claims that they were also carrying 'non-essential' ice-cream and crisps were later vigorously denied by the navy). The first trips were to Coll, Tiree, Barra and South Uist.

On the same day, the NUS General Secretary, Bill Hogarth, said the union did not regard the move as intervention in the strike, but warned that, if merchant ships were moved by naval personnel, they would be boycotted by the union.[62]

The Prime Minister, Harold Wilson, recalled in his memoirs: 'Even the mild Mr Hogarth . . . was making militant speeches and threatened me that if naval vessels were used to move strike-bound vessels to make room for incoming ships, it could mean the downfall of the Labour government. We remained ready to use the navy if it became necessary.'[63]

The more militant Scottish strike committee of the NUS confirmed on 20 May that it too did not regard the navy's action as strike-breaking; by then there were five warships operating.

A state of emergency was declared on 23 May, lasting until 6 July. Harold Wilson said: 'The government must protect the vital interests of the nation: this is not action against the National Union of Seamen'.[64]

In the event no use was made of the emergency powers. The nearest the government came to this was with the establishment of Port Emergency Committees under the regulations on 22 July, where representatives of the government, port authorities and ship owners (but not the union) were empowered to run the major ports, using troops if necessary.

Plans to use RAF transport planes to carry important industrial exports, an extension of the navy's services to other Scottish islands and preparations to fly parcel post to and from Northern Ireland were announced by Wilson in the Commons on 20 June.[65] It was also in this speech, primarily announcing the renewal of the emergency powers, that Wilson made his well-known attack on alleged communists in the NUS. His inflammatory speech apparently helped to give the moderate leadership of the union confidence to regroup and bring the strike to an end a few days later.

The government reacted strongly to the 1966 strike because it saw the dispute as a challenge to its long-term economic policy. The bitterness of the dispute also appeared to undermine some of the sympathy many trade unionists felt for the Labour government, opening the way for the increased militancy against government pay policies in the late 1960s.

Changing the Law: The Emergency Powers Act 1964

By 1964, the contingency planners had nearly two decades experience of administering an operation which, until the Second World War, had been a virtually unknown occurrence: the peaceful substitution of troops for striking workers. In those 19 years, both the pragmatically developed, post-war contingency planning apparatus and the pre-1945 laws governing MACM had been shown to be at least adequate for the military's new industrial role, as long as no constitutionalist examined them too closely.

At the end of 1964, however, the most commonly used MACM law, the 1939 Defence Regulation, was due to expire. In June of that year, the Douglas-Home Conservative government made its Regulation Six permanent by passing the Emergency Powers Act

1964. The Act is discussed in detail in chapter two. Although the implications are very significant, the passing of the Act was not a landmark in the development of MACM because the most important part of the law had been in existence, and in operation since 1939.

References

1. Lord Moran, *Winston Churchill: The Struggle for Survival 1940-65* (1966), p.286.
2. Sir Francis de Guingard, *From Brass Hat to Bowler Hat* (1979), p.46.
3. *Ibid.*, p.47.
4. *Manchester Guardian,* June 1950 (precise date unknown).
5. *Daily Worker,* June 1950 (precise date unknown).
6. Keith Jeffery and Peter Hennessy, *States of Emergency* (1983), p.238.
7. The information in this section is drawn largely from Jeffery and Hennessy, *op. cit.*, pp.181-221.
8. *Ibid.*, p.151.
9. *Ibid.*, p.220.
10. *The Times,* 14 May 1945.
11. *The Times,* 20 July 1945.
12. *Labour Government versus the Dockers* (Solidarity Pamphlet No.19; 2nd edition 1966), pp.2-5.
13. Jeffery and Hennessy, *op. cit.*, p.155.
14. *The Times,* 18 November 1945.
15. Interview with Ian Cobain, April 1982.
16. *The Times,* 11 January 1947.
17. *Army Quarterly,* April 1947, p.6.
18. CAB 134/179, EC(0)(51)21.
19. *The Times,* 13 and 14 January 1947.
20. *The Times,* 16 January 1947.
21. *Army Quarterly,* April 1947, p.6.
22. *The Times,* 29 June 1948.
23. *The Times,* 30 June 1948.
24. *Ibid.*
25. *Review of the British Docks Strike 1949,* Parliamentary Papers, Vol.XXIX, Cmd.7851 (1949).
26. CAB 134/176, EC(49)2.
27. *Labour Government versus the Dockers, op. cit.*, p.9.
28. *Ibid.*, p.10.
29. *Review of the British Docks Strike 1949, op.cit.*, p.45.
30. *Ibid.*
31. *Ibid.*
32. CAB 134/176 EC(49)16.
33. CAB 134/176 EC(49)17.
34. *Daily Worker,* December 1949 (precise date unknown).
35. CAB 128/17, CAB 24 (50).
36. *Daily Worker,* 29 April 1950.
37. *Report of the Committee of Enquiry into Stoppages in the London Docks,* Ministry of Labour, May 1951.
38. CAB 134/178, Meeting 16 May 1940.

39. *Ibid.*
40. CAB 134/137, EC(M)(50)3.
41. CAB 134/178, 30 June 1950.
42. CAB 134/177, EC(M)(50)6.
43. *Daily Worker,* 5 July 1950.
44. CAB 134/168, EC(O)(50)5, dated 11 May 1950.
45. *Ibid.*
46. CAB 134/178, EC(O)(50)11, dated 20 December 1950.
47. OCE minutes, CAB 134/178, meeting 15 August 1950.
48. CAB 134/178, EC(O)(50).
49. *Ibid.*
50. *Ibid.*
51. CAB 134/178, EC(O)(50), dated 3 November 1950.
52. *Ibid.*
53. CAB 134/179, EC(O)(51)3.
54. CAB 134/179, EC(O)(51)1.
55. CAB 134/177, EC(M)(57)4.
56. CAB 134/179, EC(O)(51)5.
57. CAB 134/179, EC(O)(51)5.
58. *The Times,* 30 May 1955.
59. *The Seaman,* July 1960.
60. *The Times,* 18 July 1960.
61. *The Times,* 16 May 1966.
62. *The Times,* 19 May 1966.
63. Harold Wilson, *The Labour Government 1964-70* (1971), p.231.
64. *The Times,* 24 May 1966.
65. *Hansard,* 20 June 1966, cols.40-41; Wilson, *op. cit.,* p.235.

Four

1970-1974

Nearly two decades of relative industrial harmony ended in the late 1960s when first the 1964-70 Labour government and then its succeeding Conservative administration tried to enforce strict incomes policies which held wage increases below the level of inflation. Inevitably, both governments clashed with a trade union movement that had become increasingly confident and powerful. 'The intensification of labour disputes and industrial strife [under the 1970 Conservative government] was the product of a variety of factors. . . . The fundamental cause, however, was the government's policy of confrontation as a means of limiting wage disputes. Strikes by local authority manual workers, the dockers and in the electrical power industry were all due to this policy. All this was made worse . . . by the rapidly rising level of unemployment. Added to all these factors, after 1972, was industrial action in protest against the government's prices and incomes policy.'[1]

This industrial action culminated in the 1973-4 miners strike which finally forced the Conservative government out of office. Troops were not used in this or the other serious miners strike in 1972, however, because the military do not possess the large numbers of skilled personnel needed to run the mines. (No government has in fact tried to send troops into the mines. Only a handful of Royal Engineers may have any mining knowledge, while tens of thousands of experienced people would be needed to produce a significant quantity of coal. Today large stockpiles of coal are held in reserve by the Central Electricity Generating Board to reduce the effectiveness of any miners strike.)

Confrontations between the Conservative government and the trade union movement were frequent and often bitter between 1970 and 1974. Legislative attempts to curb trade union power through measures such as the Industrial Relations Act 1971 were effectively nullified by radical union action. States of emergency were declared during five major disputes: the 1970 and 1972 dock strikes, the 1970 electricity supply workers overtime ban, the 1972 miners strike and the 1973-4 energy crisis and miners strike, in efforts to defeat the unions involved. Troops were mobilised in four disputes: the

1970 Tower Hamlets refuse collectors strike, the 1970 electricity supply workers overtime ban, the 1972 dock strike and the 1973 Glasgow fire brigade strike. The first three of these mobilisations were relatively minor attempts to alleviate some of the effects of the disputes, but the last, in Glasgow in 1973, was a full-blown attempt to break the strike.

1970: Dock Strike

The first national dock strike since 1926 started on 13 July 1970, less than four weeks after the Conservative government took office on 18 June. The dock workers were seeking higher wages and, having rejected the government's four per cent offer, had called a strike for 13 July. A slight increase on the four per cent just before this date led TGWU General Secretary Jack Jones to recommend the postponing of the strike but 30,000 of the 47,000 dockers had come out on unofficial strike by 14 July and on the following day a special delegate conference of the union made the strike official.

The government did not hesitate to declare a state of emergency. The Queen flew back from Canada on Thursday 16 July, and 'within 10 minutes of arriving at Buckingham Palace'[2] had signed the proclamation declaring the emergency. Simultaneously wielding a carrot and a stick, the government announced the immediate setting up of an inquiry into the dispute while saying that 36,500 troops were standing by for duty in the docks.

The government made it clear from the beginning that it was prepared to use the armed forces: 'Troops will be used in the docks if it is necessary to maintain essential services', Home Secretary Reginald Maudling stated on 16 July.[3] 'The actual timing and use of them will depend on the requirements of the port emergency committees which will be set up under the regulations', he continued.[4]

Troops stood by that weekend to move perishable cargoes but there was no military presence in the docks 'except for a few reconnaisance visits by officers.'[5] Port emergency committees were set up as in the 1966 seamens strike (see page 108).

The government withheld the troops, however, while the outcome of the inquiry was awaited. Its report, published on 27 July recommended a slight improvement on the previous employers' offer, amounting to a seven per cent increase and a conference of dockers voted to accept it on 29 July. The state of emergency was ended on 4 August.

1970: Local Authority Manual Workers Strike

Troops were first used by the Heath government during the local authority manual workers strike in October 1970.

While the July dock strike was in progress, the leaders of the 750,000 local authority manual workers were negotiating for a 55s. a week pay increase. The failure of these talks prompted a strike warning from the workers on 25 August, which the government replied to on 5 September with the threat of emergency powers. Unofficial stoppages followed and, from 27 September, selected official actions started, until by 5 October all areas of the country were hit. Refuse collectors, ambulance crews, sewerage and cemetery workers and some hospital staff were those principally involved.

The government, as in the dock strike, quickly made clear its intention to use troops if necessary. As early as 2 October, units of the Royal Engineers were reported to be ready to deal with any sewerage breakdown.[6] The Greater London Council exacerbated the situation in London by drawing up a list of volunteers from its staff to operate the London pumping stations.

There was no military intervention in the early stages of the dispute but by the second week of October the government was claiming that there was a serious threat of London's drinking water becoming contaminated through the possible breakdown of sewerage purification plants feeding into the Thames at Swindon and Reading.

On 20 October, Reginald Maudling, the Home Secretary, announced that troops had been made available to the local authorities at Swindon and Reading following the rejection by the union of the government's plea for a return to work at the two plants. A Home Office statement stressed that the Home Secretary would not wait for local authorities to appeal for service help if Department of the Environment experts believed the Thames to be dangerously polluted; i.e. the government would send in troops in contravention of even its own interpretation of the constitution.

The government said that the situation was serious and that the troops might have to be used at Swindon or Reading within a few days. The Town Clerk of Reading, W.H. Tee, stated, however, that his authority had made no request for troops and that the Reading works could possibly continue for weeks. 'The government have made their statement without consulting us', he said.[7] On 21 October the army announced that 12 soldiers were on standby at their Larkhill base to take over the Swindon works if needed.

This provocation by the government over the question of the Thames sewerage works only made the employees more determined in their strike.

One of the NUPE officials directly involved in this incident, Bernard Dix, later recalled: 'Within three days of the strike in 1970 we were called up before the Lord President of the Council, who was William Whitelaw, who said that if we didn't put people back on sewerage work they would have to call in the troops. We told them they could call in who they liked.'[8]

The troops were never used on sewerage work but the one place they did intervene in the strike was in Tower Hamlets, where the borough's Medical Officer of Health declared that some of the mounting piles of uncollected refuse on the streets were a health hazard. The Labour-controlled council appealed to the Home Office for help and their request was passed on to the Ministry of Defence. At 2.00am on Saturday 24 October an army convoy of 18 vehicles (including two mechanical shovels and a dozen tipper trucks), with 30-40 Grenadier Guards and Royal Engineers, moved into Tower Hamlets to clear away the worst five of the 18 major rubbish dumps. They did not attempt a general clearance of the refuse.

The local authority staff responded to this military intervention with a full stoppage of all work in Tower Hamlets from 26 October, and the following day the borough council met their claim in full.

A committee of inquiry under Jack Scamp was set up by the government on 25 October and its report on 5 November recommended a 50s. increase. This was accepted by the strikers and their employers but deplored by government ministers.

1970: Electricity Supply Workers Overtime Ban

A work to rule and overtime ban by electricity generating station manual workers started on 7 December 1970, the day before a major national one-day strike against the Industrial Relations Bill. The electricity workers were seeking a 25-30 per cent pay increase, but had been offered only ten per cent.

The effects of their action were felt immediately, with a state of emergency being declared in Northern Ireland late on the first day. There was a three per cent cut in power supplies at the evening peak time on 8 December and the Queen was forced to take tea by candlelight in Buckingham Palace.

The army intervened in this dispute on 8 December with the loaning of about 80 generators to badly affected hospitals in London, Newcastle, Liverpool, Sheffield, Leeds and South West England.

The Secretary of State for Trade and Industry, John Davies, set up a permanently staffed control room in his department to oversee emergency plans but told the House of Commons that troops were unlikely to be used to run power stations: 'It is not practical', he said.[9]

By Wednesday 9 December most of industry was at a standstill. Talks on 11 December broke down and a two-hour Cabinet meeting the next day at 10 Downing Street decided to proclaim a state of emergency; the Queen issued the proclamation later that same day. On 14 December Employment Secretary Robert Carr announced that the electricians union, led by Frank Chapple, had agreed to call off the action while a court of inquiry under Lord Wilberforce considered their claim. On 10 February 1971 Wilberforce came out in favour of the government's offer and the union leadership then accepted it. On 14 December Douglas Hurd, then Political Secretary to the Prime Minister and a clearly unhappy witness of the government's ineffectiveness, had sent a memo to Edward Heath suggesting that the practical side of the contingency arrangements be reviewed and that something be done to improve the Emergencies Committee.[10] It was to take the shock of the 1972 miners strike to force any change, however.

1972: Miners Strike

The miners strike of January and February 1972 was one of the most important of the 1970s and had a profound, long-term impact on state contingency planning. But there was no actual military intervention in it, as troops could not replace the strikers. The strike involved a complete stoppage in the coal industry from 9 January to 28 February when Britain's 280,000 miners staged their first national official strike since 1926. The strike, in pursuit of a 47 per cent wage claim, was preceded by a national overtime ban from 1 November.

For one month, the government did very little to conserve coal stocks, until the Cabinet Emergencies Committee on 8 February decided to declare a state of emergency. As the Queen was out of the country, a Council of State on 9 February issued the proclamation and two orders were brought in enabling the government to make power cuts and to limit the use of power supplies by banning floodlighting and advertising. By then, however, it was effectively too late as most of the coal stocks had been used up. The next day, 10 February, the government witnessed an event that is now part of trade union folklore: the closing of the gates of the Saltley coke depot by massed pickets, preventing access to one of the few remaining large stocks of fuel. Rumours circulated at the time, and subsequently, that the army was standing by to intervene at Saltley but not as strike-breakers.

They would have been helping the police maintain public order, a role they had not played in Britain in peacetime since 1926.

It appears, however, that the armed forces were not actually used at all in the 1972 miners strike. The Secretary of State for Trade and Industry, John Davies, said on the BBC TV programme '24 Hours' on 11 February that it would be 'highly unwise' to send in troops at that time.

On 10 February a court of inquiry was set up, again under Lord Wilberforce, who, from the government's point of view, had brought the 1970 electricity supply workers dispute to a satisfactory conclusion. His report was published on 18 February, by which time there were 1.6 million workers laid off because of the strike. This time, however, Wilberforce found in favour of the workers and broadly supported the miners claim. The dispute came to an end with the emergency powers finally being ended on 3 March.

The Machinery Changes Gear: From the Official Committee on Emergencies to the Civil Contingencies Unit

The Heath government received severe blows to both its economic policies and its self-esteem at the hands of the miners in 1972. But why had the disaster happened?

'Conventional wisdom in Whitehall has it that central government's handling of the 1972 miners strike was a shambles, that the old Emergencies Organisation, as developed in the late 1940s, had rusted throughout the 1950s and 1960s, and finally fell apart when required to tackle the economic and physical consequences of Mr Scargill (co-ordinator of the miners' mobile pickets). This view is directly challenged by some of the excellent officials who were involved in it throughout the period. The "shambles" story, they claim, was put about by the Cabinet Office, who took over responsibility for civil emergency planning in the aftermath of the 1972 crisis, in order to justify their imperialism at the expense of the Home Office. The real reason for the move, according to this school of thought, was the difficult relationship between the Prime Minister and his Home Secretary, Reginald Maudling. Heath wanted to by-pass a colleague in whom he had lost confidence.'[11]

Even if the old Official Committee on Emergencies/Ministerial Emergencies Committee system was not an actual 'shambles' it had not provided the Cabinet with an adequate advance warning of the 1972 miners strike and Heath therefore ordered a fundamental review of state contingency planning, encompassing all possible threats to a government's authority. Lord Jellicoe, then Lord Privy Seal, and Sir John Hunt, then a Cabinet Office Deputy Secretary, carried out the review. One of the recommendations of their report was that the old emergencies organisation should be removed from Home Office control, be revamped into a sleeker model and be based in the Cabinet Office under the close eye of the Prime Minister. Thus was the Civil Contingencies Unit born in the spring of 1972.

The first secretary of the CCU, Brigadier Richard Bishop, who held that post until his death in 1981, spent his initial months in office drawing up a list of essential industries and services most vulnerable to union disruption: 'By early 1973 ministers had detailed estimates of 16 key industries, their capacity for disruption, their importance to the country's well-being and the possibility of using alternative military labour in the event of strikes.'[12]

The CCU has always been a secret organisation. It was kept well out of the public eye for the first years of its life and its actual existence was still being officially denied 10 years after it was set up. From 1972 to 1974 there was serious industrial and social conflict inside Britain and any visible government moves to tighten internal security or bring to Britain the kind of security measures then being imposed on Northern Ireland would have been politically highly contentious. Few people therefore came to hear of the CCU until the late 1970s, and details of its work during the last part of the Heath administration are not known. It can be assumed, however, to have played a significant part in advising the government on the options open to it in the disputes of 1973-4 detailed below (see pages 66-9 for a description of its current operation).

1972: Dock Strike

Widespread discontent amongst dock workers in the early 1970s culminated in a three-week official national strike from 28 July 1972. The strike was over the future shape of the industry and the existence of their jobs: 'The dockers were faced not with a simple technological threat to their jobs, but with a conscious attempt by employers to remove the labour-intensive element in container work away from the port areas, and therefore out of the orbit of the Dock Labour Scheme. . . . The issues on which the dockers of all the major ports found common ground in the 1972 disputes — containerisation and unregistered ports — have a common origin in the determination of employers to reduce their dependence upon the registered dock workers.'[13]

The run-up to the strike began with the fining of the TGWU on 29 March for contempt of the National Industrial Relations Court over union blacking of containers in Liverpool. The tension steadily increased and, when five dockers (the 'Pentonville Five') were sent to Pentonville Prison on 21 July for their picketing activities, the TUC threatened to call a one-day general strike. This prompted the speedy release of the jailed dockers on 26 July, but by now an all-out strike was almost inevitable. A joint special committee on the docks, under Lord Aldington of the Port of London Authority and TGWU General Secretary, Jack Jones, had reported on 24 July that the two sides had reached an agreement but a special conference of the TGWU rejected the plan and the strike started on 28 July.

The government declared a state of emergency on 3 August. In order to complete the formalities for the declaration, Robert Carr, as Lord President of the Council and Home Secretary, and three other Privy Councillors had to fly to the Inner Hebrides and then be taken by boat to the royal yacht *Britannia* where the Queen, who had to sign the declaration, was holidaying. Forty regulations were made under the emergency powers but the first real use of them came with the setting up of 12 local port emergency committees on 4 August to oversee the docks and, if necessary, control them.[14]

The Home Secretary, Robert Carr, assured MPs on 8 August that 'the regulations are not directed against the dockers or their union. Their purpose is not to break the strike. It is to protect the life of the community.'[15] Whether the first of the two recorded instances of MACM in this dispute can be called protecting the 'life of the community' is open to question however. This was in Dover, where the parade ground of the Connaught Barracks was lent to the Dover Harbour Board as a sorting area for lorries seeking ferry berths to the continent. Dover was still operating because it was a 'roll-on, roll-off' port, and therefore excluded from the dockers action, but the Harbour Board had given the TGWU a guarantee that only lorries normally using Dover could be carried. Connaught Barracks was used to sort the normal vehicles from those diverted from other ports.

The second case of military assistance in the strike came with the transporting of emergency supplies by the RAF and army to Scottish islands cut off by the strike. On 10 August the Scottish Office announced that, following requests by the Orkney and Shetland county councils, the RAF would fly supplies of food for people and animals from RAF Kinloss to the islands, with chartered commercial aircraft carrying fuel in a similar operation to the Western Isles. The airlift from Kinloss began on 11 August, with an RAF Hercules flying eight tons of supplies northward. There were three more flights the next day and five more on 14 August when the operation ended, 72 tons of goods having been transported. The island of Tiree also received the services' assistance on 14 August when an RAF Andover flew in food and fuel. At the same time, an army landing craft shipped 60 tons of supplies to the Western Isles.

The Aldington/Jones committee had continued to meet all this time, however, and made sufficient progress to justify the recalling of the TGWU conference on 16 August. The conference accepted the compromise that had been worked out and called off the strike, although some rank and file resistance to what was seen as a sell-out led to its unofficial continuation for a few days longer.

1973: Glasgow Fire Brigade Strike

The first attempt since 1953 to replace completely a striking civilian workforce with troops came during the Glasgow Fire Brigade strike in October 1973. The CCU's unusual success in this operation considerably boosted the confidence of the operators of the newly revamped emergency planning organisation, in this their first real test.

Seven years later the then head of the army, General Sir Edwin Bramall (and from 1982 as Chief of the Defence Staff, head of all three armed services), described the conditions for military intervention in Glasgow as 'just right'. He went on:

'It was the first ever Fire Brigade strike in the UK. It had been condemned by the TUC and the Scottish TUC. There was little outside support; most important of all, 60 officers remained on duty and the strikers announced that their pickets would not harass either their officers or those of other fire brigades or the troops. Nor did they. And on the services' side, there was ample warning to prepare and gather together the equipment, and there was also proper service expertise, particularly in the Royal Navy and RAF. The result was that 70 to 80 calls a day were coped with over a ten-day period; and it all ended in something approaching euphoria, with special letters of thanks and free beer all round.'[16]

The Glasgow strike was unofficial, the 660 men coming out on 26 October principally in pursuit of a £5 per week pay rise but also in protest at their poor general conditions. The Fire Brigades Union at once sacked its Glasgow area executive for not preventing the strike; the General Secretary, Terry Parry, said: 'It is not a question of not supporting this strike. We oppose it.'[17]

The government ordered the troops in immediately. On 28 October nearly 70 troops from all three services took over 15 of Glasgow's fire stations, in marked contrast to the 1977-8 national fire brigades strike when this move was considered provocative and military bases were used as the operational depots instead.

Although strongly opposed by the union executive, the Glasgow strikers clearly attracted widespread sympathy from the rank and file of the FBU, some of it manifesting itself in limited industrial action. A special conference of the FBU on 29 October, called to discuss the current national pay claim, saw strong support from the delegates for the Glasgow strikers, although the executive's motion telling the men to 'Pick up the money, resume work and get the troops out' was finally carried 20,000-12,000 on a card vote.[18] The same day Cardiff Fire Brigade started providing only emergency cover until the troops left Glasgow.

The strike ended on 5 November, following an agreement three days before giving the strikers a reasonable increase. The action of the Glasgow strikers set the tone of the national fire brigade pay and conditions negotiations later that month, resulting in a substantial cut in hours and a wage rise all round.

1973-4: Miners Strike

The 1974 miners strike brought down the Heath government, led to the activation of the Home Defence emergency government system, saw the longest state of emergency since the 1926 General Strike, 'coincided' with the first modern use of troops to aid police, and prompted army discussions on military intervention in the ensuing political chaos. But there was no use of troops to maintain essential services or to break the strike more directly as in the nearest comparable situation, the General Strike, probably because troops are not capable of taking over the very large and complex mining industry.

The run-up to the emergency began when the Yom Kippur War in October 1973 led to the trebling of oil prices. This considerably exacerbated the effects of the miners overtime ban that began on 12 November, primarily in pursuit of higher wages, but also in part a political action against the policies of the Heath government. A state of emergency was declared the following day and the government denied in the ensuing debate that uncertainty over oil supplies would have led independently to the declaration of an emergency.[19]

Within a few days, however, the government had to take steps to control oil distribution. The Fuel and Electricity (Control) Bill was introduced, becoming law on 6 December. This, in many ways, by-passed the provisions of the Emergency Powers Act 1920, giving the Secretary of State for Trade and Industry temporary, but unlimited, power to control the production and supply of fuel and electricity without seeking emergency powers or parliamentary approval. The provisions of this Act were extended to November 1976 when they were replaced permanently by the coterminous 1976 Energy Act. It is now possible, therefore, as Gillian Morris says, 'for the government to use the Energy Act as an alternative to the Emergency Powers Act in the case of industrial disputes affecting energy supplies, where no further powers are required beyond those provided by the 1976 Energy Act, so avoiding the political odium of declaring a state of emergency.'[20] It appears that no further use of the emergency regulations issued under the EPA was made once the new Act was in force, with orders already made being revoked and reissued under the 1973 Act.

Petrol ration coupons were issued in November, although never brought into use and restrictions on electricity supplies for business premises began on 17 December, resulting in the introduction of the three-day week for much of industry on 1 January 1974. Railway workers also began taking industrial action.

The *Sunday Times* later claimed that in December 1973 the government 'alerted the alternative government that takes over the running of Britain in an extreme national emergency . . . The regional seats of government . . . were prepared for action.'[21] If this is true it is the only known example of the full Home Defence system, set up after the 1972 miners strike, being activated.

In January 1974, the Heath government took another step unprecedented in recent years, when it deployed troops in armoured vehicles at Heathrow Airport, reportedly assisting the police in a 'terrorist alert'. This form of military aid to the civil power (MACP) had not been seen in Britain since the General Strike. The government claimed that Palestinian guerillas were intending to shoot down an airliner; *The Guardian* said it was 'basically a public relations exercise to accustom the public to the reality of troops deploying through the high street.'[22] Whatever the truth of the matter, the Heathrow incident was seen by many as tantamount to military intervention in the prevailing industrial and political conflict.[23]

All this time there had been attempts to settle the miners dispute before it became a strike but when TUC talks broke down on 4 February the miners finally came out. On 7 February Heath called a general election for 28 February, where the Conservatives were narrowly defeated. The state of emergency ended on 11 March.

It emerged later that 'fairly senior' army officers had been talking about the possibility of some form of military intervention in civilian affairs at this time. Lord Carver, Chief of the Defence Staff in 1974, said in 1980 that he personally 'took action to make certain that nobody was so stupid as to go around saying those things.'[24] Carver is also reported to have used his influence and reputation to halt the move by army officers towards the formation of right-wing paramilitary organisations.[25]

Although Britain in the winter of 1973-4 seemed to be close to a general strike, the government mainly used political methods to try to end the crisis; no attempt was made to ameliorate the effects of the emergency by using troops to replace strikers or maintain essential services. This can probably be explained by the extreme difficulties involved in using troops and by Heath's personal determination to find a political solution to the dispute.

The possibility of using troops to transport coal was raised in late January, however, when the Vice-President of the NUM, Mick McGahey, was reported as having said he would ask any troops sent to distribute coal not to do so. In the resulting controversy he claimed he had been misrepresented: 'I would not ask one single soldier to countermand an instruction he received. The miners will not fight at someone else's expense.'[26] The Commanding Officer of an army infantry battalion reportedly said: 'Give me the chance to go and pick up Mr Michael McGahey and if it turns out to be my last assignment in the army I should die happy.'[27]

From Heath to Thatcher

In the aftermath of this crisis there was considerable debate about the extent of Mr Heath's personal responsibility for what had happened.

The Sunday Times in a major series two years later[28] believed that the Conservatives' defeat by the miners was fundamentally Heath's fault; 'Ted Heath beat himself' was their conclusion, in which they summarised popular feeling. A special Conservative Party report, prepared in mid-1977, however, believed that this was not the case. A small group of former ministers and party advisors carried out an investigation into whether or not a future Conservative government would be able to defeat striking key workers like the miners. The group, led by Lord Carrington, concluded that it would not. 'The predominant theme of the Carrington report is its warning to Mrs Thatcher that it was not the political incompetence of her predecessor that lay behind the Tory trauma four years ago. Strong unions and the advanced technology operated by their members, particularly in fuel and power industries, mean that no government these days can "win" in the way Mr Baldwin's Cabinet triumphed during the General Strike of 1926 by maintaining essential supplies and services.'[29]

Carrington took evidence in strict secrecy from prominent business people and former civil servants and their views are said to have 'opened the eyes of some of the more hawkish Tories involved'. Lord Carrington's group also examined the possibility of using the armed forces to break strikes. 'It concluded that such a practice could not be adopted on any large scale for two reasons: first, that Britain no longer had enough troops, and second, that it would permanently damage the fabric and practice of the country's politics.'[30] The firemens strike of late 1977, the largest military strike-breaking operation of recent years, indicated that the Carrington report might be wrong on these points, however — at least when Labour was in power.

Publication of details of the report in *The Times* caused 'private consternation' among the Conservative high command. The Labour Chancellor of the Exchequer, Denis Healey, described *The Times* story as 'the most disturbing he had ever read. The committee appeared to have been set up with the purpose of organising revenge for the last Conservative administration's defeat by the miners, by using the armed forces to win a confrontation with the working people of Britain.'[31]

Six weeks after the Carrington report surfaced, another Conservative Party document on the unions was leaked. This document, drafted by Nicholas Ridley MP, looked at the nationalised industries and divided them into three categories according to their vulnerabililty to strike action. Strikes in the most vulnerable areas, he concluded, should not be fought (for details see page 75).

References

1. Alan Sked and Chris Cook, *Post-War Britain* (1979), p.297.
2. *The Times,* 17 July 1970.
3. *Hansard,* 16 July 1970, col.1737.
4. *Ibid.*
5. *The Times,* 20 July 1970.
6. *The Times,* 3 November 1970.
7. *The Times,* 21 November 1970.
8. *News Line,* 3 January 1979.
9. *Hansard,* 8 December 1970, col.251.

10. *The Times,* 22 November 1979.
11. Keith Jeffery and Peter Hennessy, *States of Emergency* (1983), p.236.
12. *The Times,* 13 November 1979.
13. Tony Topham, 'The Attack on the Dockers', in *Trade Union Register 3* (1973), p.222.
14. *Hansard,* 8 August 1972, col.1590.
15. *Ibid.,* col.1593.
16. *Journal of the Royal Society of Arts,* July 1980, p.483.
17. *The Times,* 25 November 1973.
18. *Firefighter,* November 1973.
19. *Hansard,* 15 November 1973, col.685.
20. Gillian S. Morris, 'The Emergency Powers Act 1920' in *Public Law* (Winter 1979), p.345.
21. *Sunday Times,* 22 February 1976.
22. *The Guardian,* 8 January 1974.
23. See Tony Bunyan, *The Political Police in Britain* (1977), pp.272-76, for a discussion of the legal background to the Heathrow exercise.
24. *The Guardian,* 5 March 1980.
25. *The Observer,* 4 September 1977.
26. *The Times,* 30 January 1974.
27. *Evening Standard,* 1 February 1974.
28. *Sunday Times,* 22 February-7 March 1976.
29. *The Times,* 18 April 1978.
30. *Ibid.*
31. *The Times,* 19 April 1978.

Five

1975-1983

After the fierce industrial conflicts of the Heath government, the Labour administration of 1974-9 concentrated initially on restoring the country to calm and order. For a while there was a virtual honeymoon with the trade unions and, during the first three and a half years of its life, the government only used troops once during a dispute in Britain, in the 1975 Glasgow refuse collectors strike.*

From September 1977, however, the government's increasingly tough pay policies for the public sector aroused militant action from the unions and with the revamped post-1972 contingency planning apparatus in operation, the government began to call on the troops to break certain strikes in the essential services. Between September 1977 and the general election in May 1979, the military intervened in five disputes: the 1977 air traffic controllers strike; the particularly significant 1977-8 fire brigades strike; the 1978 naval dockyard strike and the 1979 ambulance and hospital workers strikes. Also important, however, was the dramatically increased number of occasions on which troops were placed on stand-by to intervene in disputes, moves that can only have heightened the tension in the disputes and may have altered their outcome.

This greatly increased military activity in the essential services in the late 1970s was caused, in part, by the gradual withdrawal (since the mid 1960s) of the index-linked wage system in the public sector under which workers automatically received pay rises in line with those in private industry. Instead, government pay curbs were most tightly enforced on those in the public sector, a large group of workers who, traditionally, had not been militant. By the late 1970s, however, this policy had made the public sector workers almost as radical as their colleagues in the docks, transport and mines in the 1920s.

*In May 1974 there was, in effect, a general strike in Northern Ireland, called by the Ulster Workers' Council against the 'power-sharing' Executive; troops were mobilised on a large scale during the strike, but after a fortnight the government had to back down, demonstrating how ineffective military intervention was likely to be in any large-scale stoppage.

The Conservative government elected in May 1979 adopted a more confrontational attitude than its predecessor to the trade union movement, attacking many of the assumptions, mechanisms and institutions that had underpinned post-1945 industrial relations. Rising unemployment, major changes in employment legislation, alterations to welfare benefits and an ideology hostile to trade unions joined military intervention in strikes as weapons in the armoury for a general campaign to undermine the effectiveness of the unions.

Under the Conservatives, the public sector workers remained ready to oppose the imposition of government pay curbs, and the strikes that saw military intervention were mainly caused by union resistance to wage restraint. The military were in action in the 1979 and 1981 naval dockyard strikes; the 1979 industrial civil servants strike; the 1980 prison officers dispute; the 1981 and 1982 ambulance crew strikes; the 1982 railway workers strike and a merchant seamens dispute in 1983. (This survey ends with the June 1983 general election). Of these, the intervention in the prison officers dispute was the largest and that in the 1982 railway strike the smallest.

1975: Glasgow Refuse Collectors Strike

The second attempt since 1953 to replace a striking workforce with troops again took place in Glasgow, this time in March 1975, when refuse collectors came out on unofficial strike.

The strike began on 13 January over pay regrading. By the beginning of March there were claims that the mounds of uncollected rubbish were becoming a health hazard. Troops were reported to be standing by on 8 March and, as there was no progress towards settling the dispute, at dawn on Wednesday 19 March, 600 men of the Royal Highland Fusiliers from Edinburgh moved in to begin clearing the rubbish in the streets. They were met by jeering pickets at the city's three incinerators and police had to clear the roads for the army vehicles. In Tower Hamlets in 1970 the troops had cleared only certain rubbish dumps earmarked as health hazards (see page 114 above), but on this occasion they took over as much as possible of the refuse collectors' jobs.

On the evening of the day on which the army's 'Operation Slant' began, Glasgow Trades Council held a special meeting which deplored the military intervention and called for a policy of non-cooperation with the troops. The next day, hundreds of Glasgow shop stewards held a demonstration protesting against the presence of troops in their city and two of the incinerators were put out of action when incinerator workers walked out in response to the Trades Council's request for non-cooperation.

Within 15 days of the army moving into Glasgow, 80 per cent of the city's worst housing areas had been cleared of rubbish and some of the troops were withdrawn. On 4 April however, the 380 strikers voted to continue their action, and the army began using bulldozers on 7 April in a provocative move that threatened to eliminate the potential overtime pay that the strikers were hoping to earn at the end of the strike. It was said that the army could remove the whole backlog of rubbish in 26 days, a strong incentive for the strikers to settle.

On 8 April the strikers voted to go back. Two days later, Sir William Gray, Lord Provost of Glasgow, attended a special ceremony at the city's Territorial Army headquarters at Maryhill where he presented the commanding officer of the First Battalion, the Royal Scots, with a special mug and a bottle of whisky 'as a token gesture of thanks to the 2,000 men who had cleared 41,500 tons of refuse.'[1] 40,000 tons were left to clear. Glasgow Corporation made a 'substantial contribution' to the Army Benevolent Fund.

Some soldiers had apparently refused to 'break a strike by a group of low-paid workers trying to get a decent wage . . . We were taken to the notorious Military Corrective Training Centre at Colchester and forbidden to tell the other inmates the real reason we were there. Like everyone else in Colchester we were put on restricted diet, which means you're permanently hungry.' They spent their days shining walls with boot polish and performing hours of hard physical exercises. Before refusing to go to Glasgow the soldiers had been told by the commanding officer that the reason for the mobilisation was that 'a group of greedy dustcart drivers had decided they wanted more money than the country could afford and were prepared to create a health hazard to get it.'[2]

1977: Windscale Industrial Workers Strike

A rare glimpse of the potential political power of the officials of the CCU came with the unofficial action by industrial staff at the Windscale nuclear reprocessing plant in Cumbria in March 1977.

The dispute centred around dissatisfaction with management, the lay-off pay which 3,000 industrial staff had been offered and the Labour government's pay policy. Labour MP Brian Sedgemore, then Parliamentary Private Secretary to Energy Minister Tony Benn, revealed what happened at Windscale in his book *The Secret Constitution* from which the following account is taken:[3]

> 'The pickets were refusing to let nitrogen through into the plant and Tony Benn had been advised of the possibility of a critical nuclear explosion if the nitrogen which was needed to keep the atmosphere inert did not arrive . . . [The CCU] had been meeting daily to review the situation. Their plan was to break the strike with troops, thus leaving Tony Benn as a sort of latter-day Churchill.'

Sedgemore's diary entry for 10 March recalls:

> 'This is the day that the panic button was pressed. The nuclear inspector brings forward the deadline, which previously was stretching out in the other direction, for getting nitrogen into Windscale. Decisions on whether to use troops have to be taken by Saturday. The Cabinet Contingencies Unit has been meeting every day. Tony calls that nuclear inspector in for an explanation of the shifting deadline and gets an explanation of a sort. But everyone is suspicious by now.'

Benn, Sedgemore and other advisors travelled to Windscale later the same day for meetings with the union officials, management and strikers. On 11 March:

> 'At the first meeting with the management and the local nuclear inspectorate it is clear that we have arrived with a mine of misinformation on the safety aspect and have not been properly briefed on the dispute. Thackeray, the nuclear inspector, makes it clear there is *no* safety risk now and there is *not* an imminent risk . . . What we were discovering was that the management had been using safety (as well as the workers) in a nuclear plant as a bargaining weapon. But now that the minister has stepped in to exercise his statutory responsibilities they are running scared. At last they've realised that the arrival of troops to break a picket line of some 500 pickets could damage nuclear development beyond repair. It's not merely a Labour government and a Labour Minister who stand to lose heavily.'

A shop steward representing the strikers told Benn that the situation had been planned and engineered with a view to burying them in the ground once and for all. Benn's personal intervention forced the managers of British Nuclear Fuels and the Atomic Energy Authority to back down from confrontation. He instructed them to reopen negotiations and they made an acceptable offer which settled the dispute.

It appears, however, that if Benn had not taken so much trouble in this dispute and had followed the CCU's advice then troops would have been used. Exactly why the CCU concocted a false case to justify military intervention at Windscale must remain open to speculation but the probable results of that intervention would have been the discrediting of Benn in the eyes of his radical supporters, the breaking of the strike and a general intimidation of all workers in nuclear plants when it became known that the state appeared to be ready to use troops even in relatively minor industrial disputes when they interfered with the nuclear programme.

The possible use of troops at Windscale was also discussed briefly during the planning inquiry into Windscale's development proposals in 1977. Fenwick Charlesworth, senior assistant chief inspector of the Nuclear Installations Inspectorate told the inquiry inspector Mr Justice Parker that troops would be brought in if there were a major failure of water and power supplies during an industrial dispute.[4]

1977: Air Traffic Control Assistants Strike

A 'classic' case of military strike-breaking occured at 2.00 am on Thursday 13 October 1977 when 60 police officers suddenly cleared a dozen pickets from the gates of the West Drayton Air Traffic Control Centre and 12 military oil tankers driven by RAF personnel thundered into the base with diesel fuel for strike-hit generators. 'The roar was incredible — I thought the Third World War had started' said one shocked picket.[5]

Air Traffic Control assistants at the base had been on strike since the end of August over the non-payment of a two-year old agreed rise for operating new computers. The civilian assistants were employed by the Civil Aviation Authority at West Drayton (near Heathrow) to operate the computer-based London Air Traffic Control System. But side-by-side with the civilian computer was that of the military flight monitoring system known as Myriad, run by the RAF, which, according to the Ministry of Defence, was 'providing facilities which are essential for the effective defence of UK air space.'[6]

On 12 October the MoD informed the press that the strike pickets had stopped diesel oil reaching the common generators that ran the two computer systems' air conditioning, without which the computers would stop. The Ministry said about Myriad: 'If this computer stops, security would be impaired and it cannot be allowed to stop.'[7] This was the apparent reason for the dramatic pre-dawn operation.

Later on the same day Ken Thomas, General Secretary of the Civil and Public Servants Association, rejected the claim that the move was essential for defence purposes, arguing that although both computers were supplied from the same fuel tank the civilian system could be isolated from the military one. But the government had not offered to isolate the military system and keep that running. 'Military personnel are being used to break an industrial dispute', Thomas said. He stated that, without the RAF's intervention, there is no doubt that the civilian computer would have been halted.[8]

The 13 October RAF swoop brought in enough fuel to run the generators until the beginning of November. Before a second run became necessary the dispute was settled, the assistants voting to go back on 1 November.

1977: Unofficial Electricity Workers Dispute

Troops were reported to have been standing by to intervene in the unofficial dispute over pay in the electricity supply industry that started in September 1977.[9] Lack of success led to stepping up the industrial action on 18 October and, by the end of the month, there were extensive power cuts. Union leaders endeavoured to persuade the men to go back to work.[10] This was successful and normal working was resumed in most areas on 7 November, the day the Fire Brigades Union decided to strike (see next section).

Brian Sedgemore says, of the power workers dispute, that the CCU discovered during it that the CEGB 'did not consider that troops had the expertise to run or even close down the national grid in a crisis. They might even destroy it if they attempted to do so.'[11] Peter Hennessy, writing in *The Times* two years later, said 'In the autumn of 1977 the CCU commissioned Mr Richard Mottram of the Ministry of Defence to investigate the possibility of using troops [in a power workers dispute]. The conclusion was that there were not enough of them and that they were not up to it.'[12]

1977-8: Fire Brigades Strike

The 1977-8 fire brigades strike was a turning point in the development of MACM. In the largest operation of its kind in recent years, almost the entire 30,000-strong fire service was replaced for two months by 20,750 military personnel, seven per cent of the total trained strength of the armed forces. As *The Times* explained: 'At stake in the dispute, apart from the dangers to life and limb, is the future of the government's pay policy, and thereby its political credibility.'[13]

Just how much benefit the government received from defeating the FBU is debatable, but the civil and military contingency planners were delighted with the outcome of what the Chief of the Defence Staff, Sir Edwin Bramall, called an 'invaluable' operation.[14] From a practical point of view the military showed they could take over an unaccustomed national role with only a few days direct preparation and sustain it for a prolonged period. And perhaps almost as significantly, the public and strikers reacted with markedly less hostility to the use of troops than in the past, thus immeasurably aiding the policy of 'normalising' the use of troops in strikes that the contingency planners appear to have been following.

The first ever national fire brigades strike started on Monday 14 November. A special conference of the FBU exactly a week before had voted to take action (against the wishes of the executive council) in pursuit of a 30 per cent pay rise and a cut in hours from 48 to 42 per week. The CCU had been watching the dispute closely and Merlyn Rees, the Home Secretary, announced that after meeting both sides on 8 November that troops would be used if necessary: 'Plans have been prepared by central government and by fire authorities, with the services, and will be ready to be put into operation on 14 November. Emergency fire appliances are being made available to fire authorities and servicemen are being specially trained to man them.'[15] He went on to explain: '. . . what I authorised a day or two ago was for the chief executives, the chiefs of police, the chief fire officers and the local army commanders to talk together about all the problems in advance of making firm decisions.'[16] An operations control room had also been set up in the Home Office.

On 9 November the Home Office wrote to fire authorities throughout the UK telling them that '. . . in the current industrial situation in the fire service . . . contingency arrangements have been made under which it would be open to them [the fire authorities] to seek military assistance in maintaining fire cover.'[17]

All this appears to have been taking place before the local authorities responsible for the fire service — and therefore responsible by the government's own rules for asking for military assistance in their area — had requested military intervention.

It also emerged later that the government had been bending rules to avoid declaring an embarassing and emotive state of emergency.

The troops were mobilised under the authority of the Emergency Powers Act 1964[18] which permitted the troops to be used on 'urgent work of national importance'.[19] But the Queen's Regulations, the armed forces' rule book, at that time stated that troops would only be used under the Act when the emergency was 'limited and local',[20] thus reflecting the intentions of the Act's drafters. The government removed the words 'limited and local' from the Regulations on 1 June 1978 (see page 61 for details).

An MoD press officer told the author they had been inadvertently retained from earlier regulations. Another legal difficulty that was ignored at the time was the question of whether or not service personnel aged under 21 were legally able to drive the Green Goddess fire engines and other civilian heavy goods vehicles. The MoD retrospectively decided that they probably were not and the government then changed the law to permit this when another FBU strike appeared likely in November 1980.[21]

Despite not having been asked to intervene by the appropriate authorities, despite the legal question mark over the lack of emergency powers, and despite having to order under-age soldiers to drive fire engines illegally, the MoD prepared for its new role as the national fire brigade. Several days before the strike actually started hundreds of troops a day were being trained in elementary fire-fighting techniques, despite London's Chief Fire Officer Peter Darby's warning that fire protection for London would be 'completely inadequate'[22] and Rees's own admission that 'there remains serious risk of loss of life and damage to property.'[23]

Merlyn Rees later recalled: 'I knew the Fire Brigades Union very well. I said to Terry Parry [FBU General Secretary] that you do realise we'll have to put the Green Goddesses in. I decided not to put them in the fire stations but in requisitioned buildings etc. — there was no point in having a great big punch-up with the firemen. And we had to use the police communications systems. The FBU knew we were going to do this; they made no protest. It wasn't a very contentious issue at all.'[24]

Troops began deploying around the country on Friday 11 November, three days before the strike started, when some local authorities had still not asked for their help. The request from the GLC, for example, did not come until that day[25] and, as the commanding officer of the 8th Signal Regiment later recalled in relation to County Durham: '. . . there was still no formal request for assistance, but preparations went ahead' [to take over fire cover for all County Durham].[26]

It was made very clear from the beginning that the government, not the local authority employers, was going to handle this strike. The government decided to take on the FBU, and the Home Office and MoD, with the other CCU planners, worked out the overall strategy; the only local decision-making allowed was within this national framework. The government made the actual decision to use troops — as the Home Office told the author at the end of the strike: 'We invited local authorities to request the use of troops'[27] — and the government was not going to allow individual local authorities to settle with their own fire brigades independently, as happened in the 1970 local authority manual workers strike (see pages 112-4).

The CCU supervised a pyramid-like structure during the strike, with two separate command systems feeding into it, the civilian and the military. The Home Office controlled the civilian side through its national co-ordinating centre on the sixth floor of the new Home Office building in Queen Anne's Gate.

The civilian tier of command below the Home Office was at county level, where this one stratum of the post-1972 home defence system was operated for the first time on any scale. Where local political considerations allowed, the 'wartime' county control rooms were brought into use and the County Emergency Committees of councillors and officials met. These committees were, in theory, constitutionally responsible for handling the dispute with their fire brigade but in fact they acted mainly as local agents for the Home Office.[28] The county control rooms and the other operational centres were the key to the handling of the strike-breaking. Here were grouped representatives of all the involved emergency services and local government officials in radio and telephone contact with their respective headquarters.

Also in each county control was a Military Liaison Cell, commanded by an army major or equivalent from the navy or RAF. The cell was the lower link between the civilian and military command systems. The military chain, the other part of the pyramid, in this case ran from the MoD Main Building in Whitehall to the army's operational headquarters at Wilton near Salisbury (HQ UK Land Forces) and then to the headquarters of the ten geographical army districts into which Britain is divided. The army district HQs controlled all military strike-related movements in their areas, whether by army, navy or RAF. The districts sent military liaison staff to each county control to form the military liaison cell which handled the day-to-day deployment of troops in fire control and acted as the conduit for consultation between the civil and military authorities at a local level.

In practice, the county controls were mainly given over to the military, police and non-striking senior fire brigade staff. Emergency 999 calls should have been routed to the fire brigade official who, after taking police advice as to the seriousness of the call, could then ask the military to provide assistance. In practice, constitutional niceties were abandoned in favour of immediate expediency. In Durham, for example, fire calls were rerouted to the Durham County Police headquarters who directly alerted the nearest Green Goddess location and then notified the military liaison cell at the county control room.[29]

When the strike actually began at 9.00 am on Monday 14 November, Operation Digest, as the Ministry of Defence called it, swung into action. Approximately 11,000 troops were standing by to replace the 27,000 strikers, although not all these service personnel were used immediately. They were equipped with about 800 Green Goddess fire appliances, ex-civil defence machines built in the early and mid-1950s. 1,060 of them had been kept in eight Home Office bases and regularly serviced ever since. Some had been used during the 1973 Glasgow fire brigade strike but most only had a few hundred miles logged. The Green Goddesses were cumbersome, slow and prone to falling over on sharp bends, not having been designed for mobile fire-fighting but rather for pumping large quantities of water onto post-nuclear holocaust blazes.

The Home Office had decided early on that no attempt should be made by the military to use either fire brigade equipment or the picketed fire stations for fear of antagonising the strikers further, so the troops were based in Territorial Army centres and local authority accommodation and had to rely initially only on the Green Goddesses. Later, more specialised equipment, which the government initially implied was not available, was forthcoming, with experienced service teams to staff it.

The strike was almost total and remained so throughout its two-month duration. The determination of the strikers, coupled with their obvious concern over the effects of their action on the public and the merits of their cause, aroused widespread popular sympathy. A national demonstration of firemen in London on 26 November saw a petition with half a million signatures handed in at 10 Downing Street. However, faced with a reluctant union leadership, little financial backing, the TUC's refusal to support them at a meeting on 21 December and an intractable government, the strikers had to compromise. At a special conference on 12 January 1978, 70 per cent of delegates voted to accept an immediate ten per cent offer, with further increases over the next two years, plus an eventual reduction in weekly hours to 42.

A key factor in their decision to resume work on 16 January was undoubtedly the relentless build-up of the military fire-fighting capability through the strike. Within ten days of the strike starting, most of the initial batch of 11,000 troops said to have been on standby appear to have been deployed, along with 33 specialist firefighting teams equipped with foam and breathing apparatus. From then on the numbers steadily built up until by the end of the strike a total of 20,750 military personnel had been involved.[30] At the end nearly all of the serviceable Green Goddesses had been used (just under 1,000 of the 1,060).

Crucial to the military's effort was their ability to train troops in basic fire-fighting techniques. The main bases used for this were Catterick, the home of the RAF's airfield fire-fighting force, which trained about a quarter of the 20,750 troops finally deployed, and the Navy's four dockyard firefighting schools (led by HMS *Phoenix* at Portsmouth) which handled possibly one half of the total. By December the basic course had been streamlined to just four hours.

The whole operation placed a great strain on military resources, with ordinary training having to be abandoned and prisoners at the Colchester Military Corrective Training Centre even being released to take part in firefighting.

Women members of the services were also used in significant numbers during the strike, possibly for the first time in military strike-breaking. They were not allowed to fight fires but instead relieved men of more mundane or administrative duties. In Durham, for example, they ferried Green Goddesses to and from workshops, ran the Eighth Signal Regiment's operations room and carried out the routine work in the military liaison cell. As the regiment's commanding officer, Colonel D.G. Cattermull put it, reflecting the services' general attitude to women in all their roles: 'The Women's Royal Army Corps are being given tasks which are within their capabilities without their being exposed to stresses and risks which should properly be faced by men.'[31]

The day after the strike ended, the MoD summarised the statistics of breaking the fire brigades strike: 'The services attended over 39,000 incidents. Of these some 33,000 were in England and Wales, about 5,700 in Scotland and some 500 in Northern Ireland. 20,750 service personnel were directly involved, of whom 4,200 were Royal Navy, 1,350 Royal Marines, 10,000 army, and 5,200 RAF. At any one time there were about 11,000 men deployed in two shifts on actual firefighting duties; 5,000 were employed on command and control, whilst the remaining 4,750 acted as relief crews. The servicemen were equipped with just under 1,000 Green Goddesses based at some 389 emergency locations, mainly TAVR centres, but including Cadet Corps huts, police stations, a holiday camp and even Carlisle Castle.'[32] Official statistics released later estimated the total mobilised effort at 180,000 'man weeks', with another 20,000 man weeks of standby effort.[33]

One statistic the government did not know at that time was the cost in fire losses during the dispute. This only became known in August 1978, when the Report of the Chief Inspector of Fire Services for 1977 was published. The Inspector, Ken Holland, concluded that 'losses during the strike were roughly double what might have been expected had the strike not occurred.'[34]

Surprisingly, the FBU officials said nothing in their history of the strike[35] about the union's experience, not even mentioning the fact that the fire fighters had been replaced by troops! Hence they had no advice, nor could they point to any lessons, to help their fellow trade unionists in future conflicts.

Many members undoubtedly did feel aggrieved, however. Even four years after the strike the fire fighters recalled the dispute with bitterness. Four FBU members at the Bethnal Green Fire Station (including a union representative) told us in 1982:

'Bringing the troops in was just a publicity exercise, an enormous con-trick on the public just to reassure the patient that he wasn't dying. The Green Goddesses were useless. They had no equipment and no training. The government, the army and the public have no conception of what fire fighting involves. There was no fire cover, it was purely cosmetic. It prolonged the strike; it would have been cheaper to give us the money, but Callaghan was determined to break the strike. We weren't allowed to speak to the troops, couldn't get near them. I wouldn't vote Labour again. Callaghan destroyed all his support. As a member of the public I'm glad they used the army. As a fireman I'm not — my hands were tied; it put the whole public in danger. They weren't being used as fire cover, they were there to break our strike. Some of them were just kids; they could have died. They're still just cannon fodder. That's a measure of the government's determination: they would let people die. I'm less dedicated now, I won't risk my life any more. If people are involved, or if it's someone's home, OK. But I'm not going to die saving property.'[36]

The military benefitted greatly from its experience during the strike. The *Daily Mirror*'s defence correspondent Ellis Plaice reported: 'Army chiefs admit, privately, that they have gained a great efficiency in operating control and communications centres in a High Street environment which would formerly have been a political minefield. One officer said: "We have got closer to the trust of the public. If it came to tanker drivers striking or anything like that, we would feel far more confident about our arrangements." '[37]

Colonel Cattermull mused on the costs and benefits of his regiment's involvement in the dispute. On the one hand, at least 23 training courses had been delayed or cancelled. On the other they had brought great credit on the army, the very large regiment had been welded together, its versatility had been proved and 'perhaps most important of all' the teenage Green Goddess crews 'had matured almost overnight'. Altogether, he concluded, 'it was a great experience.'[38]

1978: The Threat of Military Intervention

After the 1977-8 FBU strike, the threat to use troops in industrial disputes became a more common feature of government policies, both Labour and Conservative. In 1978, it appears troops were actually used only once (in the naval dockyards strike; see below), but the threat of their intervention was reported during at least five other disputes.

How real the threats were will, of course, be impossible to determine until Cabinet records are released next century. It is also possible that the threats did not represent an increase in the number of government preparations for military interventions but rather simply an increase in the occasions on which they were reported. Brian Sedgemore writes: 'The [Civil Contingencies] Unit was constantly meeting when Labour was in power and preparing behind the scenes for troops to break strikes.'[39] It appears that, after their success with the FBU strike, the government and contingency planners were more confident about using military and occasionally more prepared to let it be known that they were considering military intervention, although this always had to be balanced against the hostile reaction that could follow such statements. The increased number of military threats was also partly a response to the increased level of trade union militancy in the public sector.

The first threat to use troops in 1978 came only a fortnight after the end of the FBU strike. Petrol tanker drivers started an overtime ban in pursuit of a 30 per cent pay rise on 31 January, to the accompaniment of newspaper reports of troops preparing.[40] On 11 February, the weekly newspaper *Socialist Worker* published the Government's secret plan for handling the situation should the overtime ban become an all-out strike. Operation Raglan involved the requisitioning of oil industry vehicles and 3,000 service personnel driving HGVs. The plan had been drawn up some weeks before by the CCU on the instructions of the Civil Contingencies Committee.[41]

In September, Basingstoke Council asked the government to provide troops to help clear the mounting piles of rubbish left uncollected by the town's refuse collectors who had come out on strike a month previously in sympathy with other striking council workers. Basingstoke's chief executive said the council had made a formal request for troops but it appears that the Government dissuaded them from insisting on mobilisation.[42]

Police and army units were reported to be standing by from midnight on 5 October 1978, to deal with the effects of unofficial industrial action being taken by a breakaway group of the Prison Officers Association. The warders were pursuing a seven-year old claim for midday break payments but the announcement of an inquiry into the issue a few days before their action started defused their militancy and the action died away after a few days. *The Observer* said that the police could have contained the situation for four to five days, after which army help would have been needed.[43] In what was possibly a reference to the same dispute, Lord Harris of Greenwich recalled during a debate on the 1980 prison officers dispute (see page 149) that: 'When I was Minister of State at the Home Office we recognised that a dispute of the present character was highly likely. With a number of my colleagues, I began to make contingency plans involving the use of both the police and the army and, if I may say so, the use of temporary prisons.'[44]

The Royal Navy nearly stepped into a dispute on the Orkney inter-island ferry service in November when seven officers went on strike over a pay demand. On 23 November *The Guardian* reported that the Scottish Office was considering using the navy to deliver emergency supplies to 10 cut-off islands.[45] The dispute ended the same day.

The remaining two threats to use troops in disputes in 1978 carried over into 1979 and are dealt with on pages 139-43 below.

1978: Naval Dockyard Workers Blacking

The Royal Navy intervened in a civilian industrial dispute in its own dockyards in July 1978 when Scottish dockers employed by the navy on the Clyde stopped work on three Polaris submarines as part of a campaign for higher wages. On 26 July the Government closed the Faslane base to the normal civilian workforce so that naval personnel, under the supervision of civilian management, could load the boycotted Polaris submarine *Revenge* with missiles and other stores. While the work, normally taking 500 men three days, was in progress, Royal Marines reinforced the base's normal security cover.

The closing of the base provoked an angry response from the workers who threatened a sit-in if the action was repeated. By 9 August Faslane was paralysed by the effects of the dispute, but management/union talks then produced a satisfactory offer for the workers and, on 14 August normal working was resumed.

1978-9: The Winter of Discontent

An exceptionally high level of trade union militancy in response to government pay and economic policies earned the period December 1978 to March 1979 the popular nickname the 'Winter of Discontent'. The Labour government faced the prospect of a whole series of strikes — in the private sector from oil tanker drivers and lorry drivers, and in the public sector from local authority workers, with specific problems from the water and sewage workers and ambulance crews. Only the ambulance dispute led to the actual use of troops (see pages 143-4 below), although there was a very unusual case of the army providing assistance to a hospital management following acts of 'industrial sabotage' by employees during a dispute.

Many of the remaining disputes were seen as sufficiently serious threats by the government to warrant making preparations for MACM, and the rest of this section details those plans. The *Daily Mail* summed up the overall position early in the period: 'The army has been told to stand by to enforce the government's pay policy.[46]

The first of the disputes the government prepared to handle was the threatened oil tanker drivers strike in pursuit of a 30-40 per cent wage claim, due to start on 3 January 1979 (coincidentally a year to the day after their previous industrial action had been due to start — see above). For a fortnight before 3 January, the drivers were treated to newspaper reports claiming that the government would break their strike with troops, following a direct warning to TGWU General Secretary, Moss Evans by the Energy Secretary Tony Benn and Employment Secretary Albert Booth.[47] *The Guardian* reported on 22 December, for example, that 15,000 soldiers could be mobilised and that 160 special military instructors would be reporting to the Army's West Moors Petroleum Centre in Dorset on Boxing Day to form the nucleus of the military's training team. An anonymous 'senior army officer' was quoted as saying 'If we're going to do it, we're bloody well going to do it well.'[48]

A week later *The Guardian* gave further details of what the MoD was calling 'Operation Drumstick', stating that a state of emergency might have to be declared. The paper's defence correspondent, David Fairhall, commented: 'So far there has been a surprising lack of political protest at the government's readiness to move the troops in', going on to say that the government had probably benefitted from 'growing military interventions of this kind.' On the local authority workers' strike that was due to follow the oil tanker drivers strike he said '. . . once again it seems to be assumed, almost as a matter of routine, that the military will be on standby.'[49]

In fact, the drivers strike never materialised on any scale. An overtime ban that had started on 17 December led to panic buying of petrol within days and the ensuing shortages caused chaos in the first week of the New Year. But the drivers then voted to accept revised pay offers of around 15 per cent (well above the government's pay norm of five per cent), and the dispute ended by 10 January. The government's emergency plans were, therefore, not needed, but a few days later Home Secretary Merlyn Rees summarised what they had had up their sleeves:

'The government were ready at any time to call on the assistance of the Services and to proclaim a state of emergency should that have been necessary. The contingency plans were kept constantly under review by Ministers. 160 service instructors were trained and 15,000 servicemen were recalled from leave over the New Year holiday period and kept on short notice. Detailed contingency plans had been prepared for requisitioning of tankers and restricting the use of fuel to priority purposes. To put the plans for requisitioning tankers into effect would have required the proclamation of a state of emergency. If necessary, parliament would have been recalled. In the event it has not been necessary to put any of these plans into operation.'[50]

The oil tanker drivers dispute ended just before the government brought in the troops but the longer-running lorry drivers strike that had started at the same time was handled in a different, less military manner. The Departments of the Environment and Transport together set up an elaborate regional emergency structure to deal with the strike and liaise with the union officials, and those worked so effectively that the military were kept in the background.

The 185,000 lorry drivers started taking action on 3 January 1979, when the employers negotiating body, the Road Haulage Association, refused to increase its pay offer from 15 per cent to at least 20 per cent. Pickets at docks significantly reduced the flow of food and goods. When the TGWU declared the strike official on 11 January, the government activated the Department of the Environment's regional emergency system later the same evening to 'deal with problems over the supply of essential services'[51] by liaising with the equivalent regional TGWU secretaries, reporting to the Cabinet and easing local transport bottlenecks. Eleven Regional Emergency Committees were designated that evening, based on the Traffic Areas of the Department of Transport, and chaired by the Department of the Environment Regional Director. The Committees met the next morning to set up operations rooms with hot lines to the TGWU, RHA, National Freight Corporation and the Department of the Environment's Emergency Operations Room in Marsham Street. Announcing these arrangements at a press conference on 14 January, Transport Secretary Bill Rodgers said: 'This is a unique occasion with no precedents. The government is in no sense a party to this dispute . . . This is an attempt to ease the situation.'[52] This system had been devised by the dozen strong joint Defence Planning and Emergencies Division of the Departments of the Environment and Transport. Overall control of the operation rested with what Rees called a 'co-ordinating committee under my chairmanship.'[53]

Before the strike was made official, the government had already drawn up a list of priority supplies to be maintained and union leaders arranged with their regional committees to allow their movement. On 15 January, Rees told MPs: 'Should these priority arrangements fail to ensure the supply of food and other necessities of life, we should be ready to call on the assistance of the services, or to proclaim a state of emergency.' In practice, the regional system and the co-operation of union officials in implementing the priority scheme worked better from the government's point of view than the use of troops or emergency powers. Rees continued: '. . . any contribution that the services could make could only provide a fraction of the goods that can be moved under these priority arrangements . . . It is clear that to proclaim a state of emergency at this stage would not only distract the armed forces from their normal duties, but would not improve the present situation.'[54]

Rees was clearly right; there was no way that the 12,000 troops with HGV licences[55] could move more than a small percentage of strike-hit goods. *The Guardian* quoted Whitehall officials as putting the figure at just five per cent;[56] in the oil tanker drivers dispute the maximum that could be maintained with troops was estimated by the government at 30 per cent.[57] Both figures were way below the totals actually achieved by non-emergency measures.

The government's low-key contingency plan for the road haulage strike was an undoubted success. On 29 January Rees could tell the Commons: 'It is working extremely well — far better than under any state of emergency.'[58] A few days later the strike was settled when the drivers accepted a revised pay offer.

To add to the government's problems, local authority manual

workers were also taking widespread industrial action at this time. The 1.2 million workers rejected the government's five per cent pay offer before Christmas 1978 and decided on taking action. As early as 11 December, troops were reported to have been alerted over the dispute[59] and on 21 December *The Guardian* said that troops were being trained secretly in West Germany to run essential services. The government, however, denied this.

Local authority manual workers held a major one-day national strike on 22 January, followed by other actions around the country, on 29 January during severe weather. Transport Secretary Bill Rodgers said contingency plans were ready for troops to grit roads if necessary.[60] Pay talks finally broke down at the end of January and 500,000 employees came out on strike in the first week of February. A revised offer of 8.8 per cent was made but rejected by the unions on 7 February. Strike action intensified and troops were again said to be standing by to clear roads on 16 February,[61] but a few days later a revised pay offer of 9 per cent was made which the unions finally accepted.

The government and CCU were particularly concerned about the prospect of a strike by the 30,000 water-workers. At that time there had not been a national water strike, but the January 1979 dispute looked as if it might become one. A strike in the water industry would be one of the most serious of all, as its effects would be felt within hours and serious risks to life would quickly appear through impure drinking water and untreated sewerage.

The government spent a considerable time considering what to do about the impending water strike[62] and appears to have decided that it could not handle a national stoppage. When pay talks broke down on 11 January the government therefore quickly came back with a revised offer of 14 per cent. This might have been agreed if it had not been for the militancy of the workers in the North West Water Authority who held out for more. Their action gradually attracted support from other areas and eventually the government had to increase their offer to 16 per cent to avoid what might have become a national strike. The dispute ended around 12 January.

Peter Hennessy later revealed in *The Times* that the North West Army District had 27 military water treatment teams on standby at Fulwood Barracks, Preston, when the North West Water Authority workers began their unofficial strike. A Defence Council Instruction had been prepared under the Emergency Powers Act 1964 and only needed the signature of two Council members for the operation to go ahead. But, Hennessy says, 'The water authorities were most reluctant to call in troops. Officials kept their talks with the military secret by meeting at a public house some distance from their Warrington HQ.' He concluded: 'The lesson . . . was that the government could "win" a long, drawn out battle with manual workers provided the dispute was local and, above all, unofficial, enabling supervisory and managerial staff to keep working with relatively easy consciences. What genuinely frightens the planners is the unknown territory of an official national water strike.'[63]

1979: The Machinery Changes Gear Again

The politicians and contingency planners faced many difficult problems during the 'Winter of Discontent' and many refinements of the emergency system were developed to meet the immediate needs. As Merlyn Rees, then Home Secretary, recalled later: 'I hotted up the system.'[64]

Many of these developments have already been described. Rees claims to have initiated personally the setting up of the regional system below the CCU. It was during this period that the contingency planners seem to have become conscious that demands for military interventions in strikes could in future be routine rather than exceptional events and that their apparatus should be adjusted accordingly. Inside the Ministry of Defence a more formal system of contacts with the civil departments and the army staffs was therefore established, by centralising MACM in a department called DS6 (see page 70).

The 1979 Conservative government almost certainly carried out its own review of the emergency system after taking office, but concrete evidence of it, or its results, have not yet come to light. No dramatic change in the system has been seen in practice however, demonstrating again the non-party political approach to the contingency planning apparatus. It also indicates perhaps that this apparatus has reached the limit of its development within its current parameters, with only minor adjustments being needed in future.

1979: Ambulance Crew Strikes

The only industrial dispute of the 1978-9 Winter of Discontent where the troops actually intervened in a strike-breaking role was that of the ambulance crews, which like the water workers action, was part of the wider local authority manual workers dispute.

Ambulance crews were particularly badly paid, with a minimum basic rate of £38.44 per week and the rejection of their claim for a two-thirds increase on 12 January led to their participation in the general local authority workers one-day stoppage on 22 January.

Such was their depth of feeling over the claim that crews in many cities (e.g. London, Birmingham, Cardiff) refused to provide even emergency cover for the day and, consequently various combinations of police, troops and civilian volunteer organisations (usually the Red Cross and the St John's Ambulance Service) provided a 999 service. In London, 50 army vehicles and 85 police vans were brought into use, with the police providing the first line of cover, backed up by the volunteer services, and troops only being summoned when these could not cope.

For the next two months there was sporadic but widespread action by the crews. By the end of January there was hardly any normal ambulance cover in Britain and, on 6 February, troops again stood by in London as the effects of a work to rule in the capital became felt. Dissatisfaction with the way the dispute was handled manifested itself in a call for a 24-hour strike without emergency cover on 20 February, in which troops, police and volunteers again provided 999 services. In London, 60 per cent of the capital's ambulance stations were closed and 42 army and six RAF ambulances and crews were brought into use. On this and other occasions, military operational liaison with the ambulance authorities was provided by a group of officers stationed in the control room of the London Ambulance Service.

The government increased its pay offer on 18 February to 9 per cent plus the promise of a pay comparability study. This was eventually to provide the basis for a return to work at the end of March but industrial action continued until then (with troops being used as necessary). By the end of the dispute, service personnel had replaced striking ambulance crews in many parts of the country.

NUPE members were angry at the decision to use troops and volunteers, although there seems to have been little hostility directed at the troops themselves. One NUPE Area Officer later said that their relations with the military crews were 'Good, harmonious, even frivolous at times.' His own attitude to the troops was 'Let them get on with it, they cannot do the job as well as ourselves.'[65]

There was much more marked hostility towards the civilian volunteer organisations, however. This was highlighted towards the end of the dispute when there was a flare-up of all-out strikes following a statement by the government that hospitals should use volunteers to overcome the effects of the NUPE action. Terry Pettifer, London Convenor of NUPE during the strike, later recalled: 'Our members didn't mind the use of troops, just the use of the voluntary services. St John's were providing real scab labour.'[66]

1979: The Disturbing Case of Westminster Hospital

An unusual and almost certainly illegal incident occurred at Westminster Hospital, London, during the local authority manual workers dispute when the army was called in by the hospital authorities to deal with an act of 'industrial sabotage'.

The hospital had been hit by a strike of ancillary workers. On 1 February, two hospital vans were left blocking the main service road with their tyres slashed, thereby preventing the delivery of supplies. The *Evening Standard* reported: 'Hospital security officer Mr Ken Ely called in the army after failing to get help from the AA, the police and ambulance men . . . Regulars from the Royal Yeomanry garrison at Westminster moved in to repair the sabotaged vans.'[67] Troops were pictured using a military forklift truck at the hospital.

This was a most exceptional and irregular use of troops, possibly being, technically, aid to the police rather than maintaining essential services. It appears to have gone unnoticed in official record-keeping. Senior contingency planners have no memory of the event, and cannot say who authorised it or whether a Defence Council Order under the 1964 Act was obtained to legalise the orders given to troops; in fact, it appears quite likely that this did not happen. This most irregular use of the military needs to be thoroughly investigated.

1979: Civil Servants Pay Disputes

Civilian workers in military establishments were replaced by service personnel during two separate pay disputes in the summer of 1979.

The first dispute started within days of the Conservative Party winning the general election on 4 May. It involved the 70,000 members of the Institute of Professional Civil Servants (IPCS), the union of the scientific and technical staff, who started taking action in mid-May in pursuit of a 30 per cent pay rise and revised comparability. By the beginning of July their work-to-rule and overtime ban had escalated to limited, selective strike action and military establishments began to feel the effects. Among those hit were the Polaris nuclear submarine base on the Clyde, the Royal Ordnance Factory at Glasgoed in Gwent, which manufactures army ammunition, and the naval dockyards.

It was the situation in the dockyards, particularly Devonport, that led to civilian strikers being replaced by the military. Contingency plans for service personnel to replace strikers were reported to be ready on 7 July and on 9 July the Ministry of

Defence admitted that 'servicemen had been drafted in to prop up naval work hit by the civil servants strike in a "few isolated cases"'.[68] The MoD refused to say what the cases were, however. The IPCS reported on the same day, that Devonport was 'almost at a standstill' and the Royal Navy said 'There is no doubt about it. This action is causing us a hell of a lot of inconvenience.'[69] In order to keep the dockyards operating, civilian ship handlers at Devonport (and possibly other ports) were replaced by naval personnel.[70]

The IPCS claimed that the strike actually had a serious effect on Britain's military capability but that a D-Notice had been invoked to restrain the media from reporting just how bad things were.[71] The dispute ended in late July when the IPCS executive recommended that the claim go to the Civil Service Arbitration Tribunal.

Military establishments were again hit by strikes just a few weeks after the IPCS action finished. Leaders of the 170,000 industrial civil servants voted on 20 August to recommend selective strike action by their members to force the immediate implementation of an agreed pay settlement that the government was trying to delay. The union leaders decided to seek 'the maximum impact as quickly as possible[72] by focusing action on certain key military areas, including naval dockyards, Royal Ordnance Factories, the refuelling of RAF planes and the Aldermaston Atomic Weapons Research Establishment. 'With a bit of luck we'll ground the Air Force' said a TGWU official after the final decision to go ahead was made on 3 September.[73]

The selective strikes began on Monday 10 September and, although they did not attract the support that the union leaders had hoped, they did immediately force the MoD to mobilise service personnel to replace certain strikers.

A 24-hour strike at the AWRE on 11 September, for example, included the civilian fire-fighting team and fire cover had to be provided by an RAF squad sent from RAF Brize Norton. At RAF St Athan in South Wales, RAF fitters took over engineering work on Phantom aircraft when the civilian fitters walked out. This RAF intervention resulted in all the other civilian staff stationed at the base joining the strike.[74] It was also reported that local management at Rosyth naval dockyard had threatened to bring in navy personnel to take over the work of striking health physics monitors.

1979-80: Further Threats of Military Intervention

The Prime Minister, Margaret Thatcher, let it be known at the end of November 1979 that the government was considering sending troops to break a picket line at the Charing Cross Hospital in London.

Engineers at the hospital had been on unofficial strike since 24 October over the dismissal of two of their colleagues and their picketing of the hospital had prevented heating oil supplies being delivered. A series of media reports about besieged, shivering patients and heartless pickets, and a 'counter-picket' by nurses and doctors on 24 November, provided the government with a suitable climate to consider using troops, and it publicised the fact in a veiled threat of taking 'whatever action is necessary'.[75]

Opposed by their union, the public, other hospital staff, the government, and faced with the intervention of the armed forces the 50 strikers went back to work on 3 December following an intervention by ACAS.

Another oil tanker drivers strike in early December 1979 brought rumours of troops standing by to intervene.[76] The Shell Company was trying to reduce the number of its employed drivers by replacing them with outside contract labour and this had led to a strike by its drivers on 1 December. For a week the strike appeared to be potentially serious, especially when Esso drivers started a sympathy work-to-rule and overtime ban on 6 December. The following day *The Times* reported that, according to a Department of Energy spokesman: 'The government is watching the situation closely. Under the Energy Act it has wide-ranging powers to protect vital supplies.'[77] As early as 11 November the CCU had alerted government departments to the possibility of this strike. The strike quickly lost its momentum, however and finally ended on 17 December without the drivers achieving their goals or troops being mobilised.

Civil contingency planners will always remember 1980 for the Prison Officers dispute when the British armed forces again demonstrated their versatility by becoming prison administrators and warders (see below, page 149). This was the only time troops were actually used for MACM during the year but on at least three other occasions it was made known that they were standing by to intervene.

The first of these was the dispute by the water workers, who, exactly a year after their last dispute, were again threatening a national strike. Leaders of the three main unions in the industry (NUPE, TGWU, and GMWU) decided on 17 January to take strike action unless the employers improved their 13 per cent pay offer (the unions' target was at least 40 per cent) and implemented the findings of a comparability study which had shown water workers to be earning £10 a week less than their counterparts in the gas and electricity industries. The union leadership was reluctant to strike, however and talks continued until an acceptable offer of 21 per cent was made on 21 February.

The CCU's plan for dealing with the water workers strike was disclosed by Peter Hennessy in *The Times*.[78] After electricity, water is the most difficult service of all for the planners to handle, particularly during a national strike. The plan indicated that troops would only be able to handle a national strike if civilian supervisory staff stayed at their posts; if they did not the position would rapidly become unmanageable, even with 15,000 service personnel deployed. In a local strike, the troops might be able to manage without supervisory staff, but in either event the planners had to face the fact that, within 48 hours of a strike starting, serious health hazards would arise. The CCU plan had been updated after the 1979 strike and the events in the North West (see page 142), and specified using 3,000 techncians, 2,200 drivers, 5,000 general duties personnel and 4,800 command and control staff. The planners hoped, however, that water workers would be deterred from taking strike action by the public opprobrium that might be aroused when health was seen to be at risk.

A non-specific threat to send troops into hospitals to break strikes of hospital workers came to light in April 1980 when the Scottish area secretary of COHSE, Keith Hickson, revealed the contents of the latest DHSS contingency plan. This had recently been revised and, in addition to telling hospital authorities to make greater use of volunteers in disputes, made clear that troops could be used as well.[79] The government later confirmed the existence of such a plan.[80] (See also page 155).

Memories of the 1977 Fire Brigade Union strike were revived in November 1980 as the Green Goddess fire engines were again wheeled out of their Home Office depots when the FBU became the first union to clash with the government over its new 6 per cent limit on local authority pay rises.

The FBU had been expecting an 18.8 per cent rise in line with the agreement worked out at the end of the 1977-8 strike, but at the last moment the government imposed its pay curb and the local authority employers who had been prepared to pay the 18.8 per cent, decided instead on 7 November to offer only six per cent. The union leadership immediately announced that its annual delegate meeting would be recalled on 21 November to vote on an executive plan for a series of one-day national stoppages. In good time for the conference, the government stated on 14 November that the Green Goddesses had been made available to the armed forces to allow time for preliminary training at seven military centres.

A government statement said: 'It does not mean that the

government regards strike action by firemen as inevitable, but in the present situation it would be irresponsible not to make preparations on a contingency basis.'[81]

The Transport Minister, Norman Fowler, also signed an order to allow service personnel to drive fire engines, hastily legalising for the future a practice that the government had been advised was probably illegal in the past. The Labour Party's chief press officer said: 'It is an important matter which, again, has been slipped through without proper debate in parliament.' (It should be pointed out that the previous Labour government had presided over the occasion of actual illegality, when under-age soldiers drove Green Goddesses in the 1977 fire brigades strike). The FBU General Secretary designate, Ken Cameron, described the government action as 'highly provocative.'[82]

Talks continued until 28 November when deadlock appeared to have been reached and definite plans for strikes from 3 December were made. Numerous newspaper reports had made it clear, however, that the troops were ready to go in,[83] although just how competent they were was questioned later when troops practising at their depot in Middlesex started a fire which spread uncontrollably and had to be put out by the local fire brigade.[84]

On 1 December, however, the basically sympathetic employers offered a two-stage version of the FBU claim which the union accepted.

1980: Prison Officers Dispute

The government's rearrangement of the law governing the age of HGV drivers for its own benefit during the Fire Brigade dispute went largely unprotested at, as it coincided with the passing of a law described by the National Council for Civil Liberties as 'one of the most dangerous laws to be put on the statute book since the War.'[85] This was the Imprisonment (Temporary Provisions) Act 1980, rushed through all its stages in parliament in just 13 hours 20 mins[86] to enable the government to break the prison officers dispute. The Act greatly extended the power of the executive over the judiciary, allowed the government to set up prisons staffed by troops and removed some of the rights of prisoners.

The dispute arose out of long-standing complaints by the prison officers (and penal reformers) that conditions in British prisons were intolerable for both prisoners and warders. Three-quarters of prisons were built in the 19th century, they were grossly overcrowded and, as a former Director General of the prison service said, 'The conditions are bloody disgraceful. Abominable.'[87] In the autumn of 1980, the frustrations felt by the members of the Prison Officers Association focused on the question on payment for meal breaks. Indefinite industrial action began on 5 October, the most potent aspect of which was the officers refusal to accept prisoners remanded or sentenced by courts. By 28 October, the day the government's sweeping new law came before the Commons, there were over 3,500 prisoners being held in police cells, many 'in conditions that are unsatisfactory in human terms and often with a lower standard of security than the public have a right to expect,' according to the Home Secretary, William Whitelaw.[88]

The formal moves to mobilise troops and introduce emergency legislation began on Thursday 23 October, after an abortive meeting between Mr Whitelaw and the POA. The Cabinet, after consulting the CCU, agreed that the Home Office should formally ask the MoD to provide military assistance. The government then let it be known to the media that, when parliament reassembled the following Monday, it would be seeking emergency powers which would include the use of army camps to house prisoners. Colin Steel, chairperson of the POA, said that if army camps were used it would be 'deliberate provocation'.[89]

On the morning of 24 October, two members of the Defence Council, General Sir Patrick Howard-Dobson (Vice-Chief of the Defence Staff) and Geoffrey Pattie (RAF Under-Secretary of State), signed a Defence Council Order authorising the use of troops under section 2 of the Emergency Powers Act 1964.

The army, however, pre-empted this order, as senior officers of the Gordon Highlanders had already been mobilised to investigate the potential of the unfinished Frankland maximum security prison near Durham as an army-run emergency overspill prison.

Lt Colonel C.H. Van der Noot of the Gordon Highlanders describes how these veterans of the counter-insurgency campaigns in Malaya, Cyprus, Borneo and Palestine came to be running a British civilian prison:

'As we prepared to go to the Sergeants Mess Dargai Ball on a Thursday in October [the 23rd] a short call from [army] HQ Scotland directed that the Battalion was to come under Command of HQ North East District from 0900 the following morning with a view to running a new unfinished Prison at Durham. Later that evening, whilst dancing the Gay Gordons with the Regimental Sergeant Major's wife, the Commanding Officer received the first of several yard-long classified signals giving the details of the operation. An early departure from the Ball ensured a prompt arrival outside the walls of Her Majesty's Prison Frankland.'[90]

The officers spent 24 October touring the prison and meeting the police, the prison governor and the staff of HQ North East District. By the evening 'we had just an inkling of the size and nature of the task in hand.'[91]

The POA also claimed on 24 October that army barracks in the Oxford, Plymouth and Preston areas were being considered as temporary prisons by a joint team of MoD and Home Office officials. An MoD spokesman refused to confirm this but said: 'Discussions and exchanges between the MoD and the Home Office are taking place.'[92]

Over the weekend of 25-6 October supplies and equipment were moved into Frankland Prison in readiness for the arrival of troops, although, as the MoD said: 'The army has not yet been asked to provide assistance.'[93]

Before the troops could become prison officers there had to be some substantial changes in the law, however, and, on 28 October a surprised House of Commons heard William Whitelaw describe the sweeping powers that the government wished to have. The Imprisonment (Temporary Provisions) Bill gave the executive unprecedented powers over the judiciary and parts of the Bill have turned out to be more permanent than MPs expected. The Bill introduced the concept of 'executive bail' to allow the government, rather than the courts, to release prisoners. The Bill also gave the Home Secretary power to designate 'any place' as an 'approved place' for the detention of prisoners; removed the guarantee that prisoners were entitled to certain statutory rights; gave the police the right to hold prisoners in police cells; and gave troops all the powers, authority, protection and privileges of a constable (while acting as warders), possibly for the first time in British history.

The section giving the police power to hold prisoners was permanent but the rest of the powers had to be renewed monthly or they would become dormant. After 12 months they would disappear altogether from the statute book unless the Home Secretary laid an order before Parliament postponing the repeal. The government gave MPs the impression that after 12 months was up, these provisions would, in fact, disappear, and Leon Brittan, Home Office Minister of State, even said 'I would not support for one second what is proposed if it were put forward on a permanent basis.'[94] But a year later, on 28 October 1981, the government successfully asked Parliament to renew its powers, saying they needed to be kept in reserve as the prison officers action had only been suspended.

The Bill received Royal Assent late on Wednesday 29 October and the Gordon Highlanders at Frankland could then get on with their new job. Lt Colonel Van der Noot describes what had been happening in the interim:

> 'The Battalion Group which started to arrive at HMP Frankland from Edinburgh [the Highlanders base] on the Monday morning was tasked with establishing, administering and providing perimeter security for the Prison. Initially the Prison was bare apart from one table and twenty-odd chairs, there were no locks and no door handles and no telephone, though happily light, heating and water. Thus, whilst the leading Company was setting up double bunks in the cells the Governor and the Commanding Officer began the task of working out joint operating procedures with a view to ensuring that the Prison was ready to receive prisoners from the Thursday morning. The Governor was assisted by 19 members of the Governor Grades drawn from all over the United Kingdom.'[95]

The MoD at first said that troops at Frankland and any other prisons would not come into contact with the civilian prisoners because they could not be sure of either the prisoners or the public's reaction.[96] At Frankland, however, Van de Noot says that it was soon realised this was not practicable and a new plan based around military staffing was devised and then modified by Whitehall so that the 'interface' troops as they were known would be quasi-legal forces (military police and prison officers).

By Thursday, 30 October, Frankland contained, besides the Highlanders, units of the Royal Military Police, the Military Provost Staff Corps, the Army Catering Corps, the Royal Engineers, the Royal Navy (medical and police), and the RAF (dog handlers and police). The first prisoners arrived at 4.00pm that day — in a bus provided by the 'Happy Holidays' Bus Company! The Governor said 'We are creating a unique piece of penal history.'[97]

By this time, work was also starting on a second emergency prison, the army camp at Rollestone on Salisbury Plain. Frankland held up to 600 prisoners and Rollestone 350; other similarly-sized military camps were to be brought into use as required.[98]

Rollestone was soon activated and from then until the end of the dispute no further military camps appear to have been needed as the government's emergency measures contained the problems stemming from the POA's action, although only at the cost of considerable hardship to prisoners.[99] The Home Office put forward a peace formula late in December which was first rejected but then, in mid-January, agreed. This led to bitter arguments and strife inside the Association which came to a conclusion in early

February when a delegate conference suspended the action.

Van der Noot, however, was delighted with his experiences at Frankland, which he describes as 'virtually being run by the Services': '. . . the Services with their capacity for and experience of dealing with the unexpected, and especially the army's recent involvement in many varied MACM operations, combined with its experience of working with people in Northern Ireland, allied to their inherent organisational structures and administrative support, were able to give confidence to the whole machinery from the outset.'[100]

Official statistics on the military's involvement in the strike showed that 1,000 service personnel were deployed for a total of 17,000 'man weeks', while an unspecified number of troops put in another 60,000 man weeks on standby.[101]

The extent to which the British army is now oriented towards operations within the civilian community is highlighted by what happened to the Gordon Highlanders soon after they had the prison running smoothly: they were ordered back to their Kirknewton base to begin training for possible intervention in the fire brigade strike. 'Within a week of handing over the gaolers' keys the Battalion was manning 50 Green Goddesses.' As Lt Colonel Van der Noot said: 'What next?'[102]

1980-1: The Strike Season

By the end of 1980 the winter period of December-March each year was so regularly seeing industrial action by a wide range of workers that the four months had become commonly known as the 'Strike Season'. The Civil Contingencies Unit had calculated before the 1980-1 season that the most troublesome threats that would have to be faced were, again, from the water workers and the oil tanker drivers. Once more, however, actual military intervention was avoided.

The oil tanker drivers dispute did not become as serious as feared but the CCU had a major problem on its hands when 'flabbergasted' union negotiators for the water workers rejected what they considerd a derisory 7.9 per cent pay offer on 6 January and the leader of the General and Municipal Workers Union team said: 'I don't think we have ever been closer to a national strike.'[103] Another negotiating meeting was fixed for 3 February but union leaders made it clear that, in the meantime, they would be seeking their members approval for a strike if the offer was not improved. The government was trying to keep public sector pay rises below a ceiling of 6 per cent but had handed over 15.5 per cent to the miners and this lesson in what could be gained from militancy was not lost on the water workers.

This was the third year in a row that a national water strike had been threatened and details of the government's contingency plans had become almost common knowledge. The media, reporting these plans, were agreed on the basics: 15,000 troops would be available with some specialist equipment; a state of emergency would have to be declared so that water authority equipment could be requisitioned but otherwise a state of emergency was almost valueless and would only buy a little negotiating time; public health would quickly be endangered; and the dispute would have to be settled in days rather than weeks. The troops might be able to handle a very localised strike on their own but for anything more widespread they were totally dependent on civilian supervisory staff (NALGO members), staying at work.[104] When the NALGO members decided not to co-operate with troops, however, the government's contingency plans, so painstakingly revised after the experiences of the previous two years, became almost worthless.

The unions did not, however, press home their advantage. Two improved offers were made at the beginning of February and immediately rejected, but no national strike action was taken. On 16 February, unofficial strike action began in north east England, followed by the first local strike in the north west (leaders of the militant action in 1979) around 23 February, and then the first move towards national action. The frightening prospect of a national strike brought the government and union leaders back to the negotiating table and, on 25 February, they agreed a 12.3 per cent deal and the strike was called off. The membership finally accepted the deal on 16 March. A national water strike had been avoided for another year.

1981: Civil Service Strikes

Military personnel again replaced civilian strikers at the Clyde Polaris submarine bases in April 1981.

Britain's 540,000 non-industrial civil servants began taking selective strike action from 9 March in an attempt to obtain a 15 per cent pay increase. Indefinite strikes at key points were started in order to apply the maximum pressure on the government while keeping a large number of the trade unionists at work to support their striking colleagues.

Military bases were a particular target, and the government was soon faced with the prospect of its strategic nuclear submarine fleet becoming strike-bound on the Clyde. On 9 April, the Prime

Minister condemned the stoppage and four days later 16 naval personnel were used at the Coulport base to re-arm the submarine *Resolution*.[105] This provoked a half-day national stoppage by the civil servants the next day. The position with the submarine deteriorated steadily after this and on 17 May, it was reported that defence chiefs were becoming increasingly concerned as three of the four submarines were then 'practically locked in their bases'.[106] The navy was using its own fleet maintenance units but the civilian specialists needed for major repairs appeared to be irreplaceable.

The civil servants strike was so prolonged and extensive that it is likely that troops carried out other, more minor, and unrecorded replacements of strikers. Known examples include a claim in March that the army had handled mail for the Inland Revenue.[107] It was also reported that the government considered using service personnel to take over air traffic control at Heathrow but finally decided against the scheme because it may have led to an intensification of strike action.[108]

The strike dragged on inconclusively, with the government taking a hard line, until the unions finally gave up their struggle on 19 July having gained little.

Ministry of Defence evidence to the Megaw inquiry into civil service pay later in December 1981, indicated that the April strike on the Clyde had in fact, hit Britain's nuclear attack capability hard, and showed that the MoD was considering replacing key civilian workers at nuclear bases with military personnel.[109] The following March almost 120 civilian jobs at Faslane were permanently assigned to Royal Navy personnel.[110]

1981: Ambulance Crew Strikes

The government's new contingency plans for dealing with disputes in the National Health Service were leaked in mid-January 1981, and then partly implemented some five months later during the ambulance crews dispute.

Work on the plans had started in 1979, following the health service disputes in the early part of that year.[111] There were actually three separate plans, each with its own codename:

Plan Lionel (after Lionel (Len) Murray, General Secretary of the TUC?) was for strikes involving 'certain skilled and semi-skilled [hospital] ancillary workers' and allowed 'limited services assistance.'[112]

Plan Concord could be activated in an ambulance crews dispute, and provided for troops to drive NHS ambulances.

Plan Bittern was an alternative to Concord, with troops using military ambulances to replace the NHS system.

In an ambulance strike ministers would decide between Concord and Bittern according to the scale of the dispute and the anticipated reaction from strikers and the public.

The three main plans were outlined in a memo to DHSS regional administrators from John Shaw, an Assistant Secretary in the contingencies and industrial action branch of the DHSS Regional Liaison Division, sent out on 19 December 1980.

The memo said: 'Any disclosure of information contained in these plans would be extremely damaging to the government's industrial relations policy. It is imperative that the "confidential" classification of this information should be strictly observed, and that its circulation should be as limited as possible on a "need-to-known" basis strictly interpreted.' The memo stressed to the administrators: 'You are in possession of military plans which are highly sensitive.'[113] The memo was leaked a few days before the ambulance pay talks were about to begin.

TGWU national officer Michael Martin said: 'They are trying to put the scares on our people. Here is a government that publicly deplores military intervention against workers in Poland and yet is planning the same thing itself.'[114]

The pay talks actually began in February, finally breaking down at the beginning of June. The union leaders then called for one-day stoppages but with emergency cover provided, thereby possibly avoiding the need for military intervention. Rank and file anger was such however, that two days before the first stoppage on 17 June, London and Scottish crews staged their own 24-hour strike without emergency cover, as they considered providing emergency cover rendered stoppages ineffective.

The government decided not to risk a confrontation with the obviously militant strikers by using Plan Concord to send troops to drive NHS ambulances and instead activated Plan Bittern. Troops and military ambulances stood by in army barracks throughout the day, but it appears that they were actually only used in one area as emergency arrangements (co-ordinated by the police) with police, Red Cross and St John's drivers coped with the 999 calls.[115]

The place where troops were used was in South Wales, in Gwent and Glamorgan, where nine RAF ambulances answered 999 calls, mainly in Cardiff.[116]

The crews' action did not have the success they hoped, and, after rather ineffective strikes in London and elsewhere on 26 June and 3 July, when again the army stood by but was not needed, the unions had to concede virtual defeat on 20 July by accepting the six per cent pay offer.

1981: The Oil Tanker Drivers Dispute

Operation Leadburn was the code name given by the planners to the contingency plan for breaking the oil tanker drivers threatened strike in November 1981.

Shell, BP, Esso and Texaco were seeking the same 11 per cent pay rise Mobil's drivers had received, rather than the offered eight per cent. The armed forces were alerted after a national strike had been fixed for 16 November, with 12,000 troops being prepared to deliver supplies to 4,000 designated service stations which would only have been able to serve 'authorised users'. A state of emergency would have been declared almost immediately.[117]

The Acting General Secretary of the TGWU, Alex Kitson, aroused passions by warning that this could actually be seen as a 'political' strike, comparing the situation that might arise with that which brought down the Heath government in 1974. Troops began training at the army's West Moors Petroleum Depot in Dorset, and it was reported on 11 November that 'The government seemed at some pains yesterday to give advance warning that it is prepared to use troops to maintain fuel supplies in the event of a strike.'[118]

The dispute came to an end, however, as a ballot of the drivers showed a majority in favour of accepting the eight per cent offer. The TGWU accepted the offer on 2 December.

1982: Rail Strike

Troops were used in a minor role during the two-day national rail strike by members of the NUR on 28 and 29 June. The strike was part of a prolonged dispute over pay that ended unsatisfactorily for the union, with the stoppage itself proving unpopular with the union members.

With NUR members in both British Rail and London Transport on strike, traffic chaos was expected in London. 'In order to accommodate the vastly increased volume of cars entering the metropolitan area, free parking was provided in the London parks. Since one of the wettest Junes in living memory had left the ground soft and deep, troops were employed to lay wire netting for the cars to park on.'[119]

The use of troops went almost unnoticed by the union in the confusion over a decision to call off the strike that came within hours of the strike starting.

1982: Ambulance Crew Strikes

Troops replaced striking ambulance crews for the third time in recent years during the long-running health service dispute over pay that started in mid-May 1982. All health service workers had asked for a 12 per cent pay rise, but the government would only offer six per cent initially. A series of local and national stoppages followed over the summer with widespread support being received from workers in other industries, particularly in the public sector.

Troops were first reported to be standing by for emergency ambulance duty during the 6 June one-day strike but police and volunteers maintained a service. The government increased its offer to 7.5 per cent but the nurses rejection of this led to the dispute becoming even more bitter. There was an intense five-day campaign of action from 9-13 August which again received substantial national support. At the end of August there was a brief flurry of interest in the possible role of troops in the dispute when the Health Minister Norman Fowler said that members of the armed forces had been, and would continue to be, on standby. The health unions interpreted this as possibly applying to jobs other than ambulance driving and Albert Spanswick, General Secretary of COHSE, said: 'If the troops are brought in there will be trouble on the picket lines.'[120]

In fact, troops were kept very much in the background throughout the dispute as police and volunteer drivers were able to maintain emergency cover. The actual military intervention in the dispute (which appeared to provoke no hostile response) was very small and came during the 22 September national day of action called by the TUC when employees in other industries were encouraged to take some form of industrial action in support of the health workers. The army had 25 ambulances on standby in London and one of these took a man who had a heart attack to hospital.

1983: Water Workers Strike

'Water supply is one of the contingency planners' most intense worries. The prospect of sewage in the streets is a politician's nightmare.'[121] In January 1983, the nightmare almost became real when manual workers in the water industry held their first national strike. Somewhat surprisingly, however, the effects were not nearly as bad as had been feared, mainly because the unions maintained emergency cover in most areas and because of the high level of automation of plant and machinery.

The strike started on 24 January after months of pay negotiations and internal deliberation. The 29,000 manual workers, mainly members of NUPE and the General, Municipal,

Boilermakers and Allied Trades Union (the former GMWU), were offered a four per cent pay rise by the National Water Council in line with government pay policy. The unions, however, were seeking a 15 per cent rise and comparability with gas and power workers in the last centrally-conducted wage negotiations before a new regional negotiating system came in, which was expected to weaken the bargaining strength of the unions.

The strike ended a month later, on 24 February after an independent committee of inquiry awarded the unions 12 per cent, but not the comparability, in what was seen as a clear defeat for the government. On the last day of the strike around 100,000 properties were without direct water supplies and just over eight million people were being advised to boil their water. But there had been no sewerage flowing in the streets and apparently no serious health problems, although some raw sewerage was being discharged into rivers.

Even before the strike started troops were reported to have been put on alert for what had been officially code-named Operation Keelman. *The Guardian* reported:[122]

'Troops will only be called in if the supply and sewage system is on the point of collapse, Whitehall sources indicated last night. Units of the armed services that might be called out have been alerted but they are not yet formally on standby. This is because the Department of the Environment thinks it would probably be counterproductive to bring in troops at an earlier stage. While supervisory staff at the water works stay out of the argument, they should be able to keep the system going on an emergency basis. But if they were to stop work, in protest at the striking manual workers being replaced by troops, the military would not be able to cope on their own. The Environment Department has learned that although the three services can between them provide several hundred engineers trained in various specialities, and thousands of unskilled men in support, they cannot be expected to run a complex system like a power station or a sewage works, with all its attendant health hazards, without professional help. All they could do is improvise some sort of emergency service.'

The government was also apparently prepared to declare a state of emergency under the Emergency Powers Act 1920. This would have given troops and water authorities power to requisition equipment, and, the *Financial Times* said: 'would give the water authorities immunity from litigation for breaches of their statutory duty to maintain water supplies and dispose of sewage. Emergency powers could also possibly strengthen water authorities' own powers by allowing them to obtain water from sources not normally sanctioned for doing so.'[123]

Neither troops nor a state of emergency were needed, however.

One consequence of the strike was to lead the Conservative government to consider introducing legislation to ban strikes in essential services. A confidential memorandum produced by the Centre for Policy Studies, a Conservative 'Think Tank', suggested that workers could be persuaded to forgo the right to strike by offering them increased pay (possibly index-linked) and improved pensions.[124] Six days later the Prime Minister, Margaret Thatcher, told the House of Commons that the government was thinking of making strikes in essential services illegal, a move possibly involving the imposition of a statutory duty to maintain such services. No concrete proposals were announced before the June 1983 General Election, however.

1983: Pirates in the Royal Navy

The last military intervention in an industrial dispute during the 1979-83 Thatcher government occurred around midnight on 31 March 1983, when the Royal Navy sailed off in a ship while its civilian crew was on holiday.

The *Keren* was a Sealink ferry that had been requisitioned by the MoD for service in the Falklands. The MoD negotiated a crewing agreement for the *Keren* with a civilian company, Blue Star, but while the ship was refitting at Wallsend-on-Tyne prior to sailing to the Falklands a dispute over pay and conditions arose between Blue Star and the Merchant Navy crew.

Faced with an unexpected increase in its costs, the MoD decided to hijack the *Keren*. In a carefully planned move carried out with the Prime Minister's knowledge[125] 55 Royal Navy personnel quietly slipped aboard the *Keren* in civilian clothes late on 31 March, a few hours after her crew had been sent on Easter leave. A secret commissioning service was then held on board to turn the vessel into a warship and hence ensure that the naval sailors had to obey orders, as laid down in the military discipline acts.

The Royal Navy crew stayed aboard unseen until early on Saturday, 2 April, when tugs were summoned to tow the ship to sea. For the next few days HMS *Keren* steamed about off the mouth of the Tyne while the navy, the Blue Star company and the National Union of Seamen argued about what had happened. After the NUS threatened to call a worldwide stoppage of British seamen talks were convened at ACAS on 5 April, resulting in the MoD making concessions that the NUS found acceptable. The *Keren* was returned to her civilian crew on 8 April.

1983: The Last Threat

Just before the June 1983 general election the government made the last of its many unfulfilled threats to use troops in a dispute.

The government came into conflict with the Fire Brigades Union because the Home Office wanted to increase firemen's pension contributions by up to £6 a week. The FBU called a delegate conference for 26 April to discuss the issue, with the union's executive recommending strike action. But, as so often has happened, a few days before the crucial meeting the government let it be known that troops were ready to intervene. The government's ageing civil defence fire tenders, the Green Goddesses, were reported to be ready for distribution to service units in readiness for any one-day strikes by firemen.

The delegate conference, however, voted against any action, and the Green Goddesses were wheeled back into storage to await the next dispute.

References

1. *The Times,* 12 April 1975.
2. *Socialist Worker,* 26 November 1977.
3. Brian Sedgemore, *The Secret Constitution* (1978), pp.98-103.
4. *The Guardian,* 17 August 1977.
5. *Morning Star,* 14 October 1977.
6. *Daily Telegraph,* 13 October 1977.
7. *The Guardian,* 13 October 1977.
8. *Morning Star,* 14 October 1977.
9. *Daily Mirror,* 15 November 1977.
10. *The Times,* 4 November 1977.
11. Sedgemore, *op. cit.,* p.142.
12. *The Times,* 15 November 1979.
13. *The Times,* 14 November 1977.
14. *Journal of the Royal Society of Arts,* July 1980, p.483.
15. *Hansard,* 9 November 1977, col.675.
16. *Ibid.,* col.677.
17. FIR/71 175/2/54, quoted by Colonel D.G. Cattermull in *Journal of the Royal Signals Institution,* Winter 1978, p.3.
18. *Hansard,* 10 July 1981, Written Answers, col.491.
19. Cl.38, s.2.
20. *The Queen's Regulations for the Army,* 1975 edition para. J11.004.
21. *The Times,* 15 November 1980.
22. *Daily Telegraph,* 11 November 1977.

23. *Hansard,* 9 November 1977, col.673.
24. Interview with the author, 9 December 1982.
25. *Daily Telegraph,* 12 November 1977.
26. Cattermull, *op. cit.*
27. Author's notes.
28. See Cattermull, *op. cit.,* p.7.
29. *Ibid.,* p.6.
30. MoD News Release 2/78, 17 January 1978.
31. Cattermull, *op. cit.,* p.9.
32. MoD News Release 2/78, *op. cit.*
33. *Statement on the Defence Estimates,* Vol.2, Cmnd.8529 (1982), p.60.
34. *Report of HM Chief Inspector of Fire Services for 1977,* Cmnd.7311 (1978).
35. *Firefighter,* February 1978.
36. Interview with Ian Cobain, March 1982.
37. *Daily Mirror,* 17 January 1978.
38. Cattermull, *op. cit.,* p.14.
39. Sedgemore, *op. cit.,* p.132.
40. E.g., *Sunday Times,* 29 January 1978; *Daily Telegraph,* 31 January 1978.
41. *Socialist Worker,* 11 February 1978; *The Times,* 10 February 1978; *Daily Telegraph,* 13 December 1977.
42. *The Guardian,* 6 September 1978.
43. *The Observer,* 8 October 1978.
44. *Hansard (House of Lords),* 18 December 1980, col.1240.
45. *The Guardian,* 23 November 1978.
46. *Daily Mail,* 11 December 1978.
47. *Financial Times,* 22 December 1978.
48. *The Guardian* and *Daily Telegraph,* 22 December 1978.
49. *The Guardian,* 29 December 1978.
50. *Hansard,* 15 January 1979, col.1318.
51. Department of Transport Press Notice No.19, 11 January 1979.
52. Author's notes.
53. *Hansard,* 15 January 1979, col.1319.
54. *Hansard,* 1 January 1979, col.1320.
55. *Hansard,* 24 January 1979, col.194.
56. *The Guardian,* 19 January 1979.
57. *Hansard,* 15 January 1979, col.1322.
58. *Hansard,* 29 January 1979, col.1042.
59. *Daily Mail,* 11 December 1978.
60. *Hansard,* 29 January 1979, col.325.
61. *Daily Telegraph,* 17 February 1979.
62. *The Guardian,* 21 December 1978.
63. *The Times,* 16 November 1979.
64. Interview with the author, 9 December 1982.
65. Interview with Ian Cobain, April 1982.
66. Correspondence with Ian Cobain, April 1982.
67. *Evening Standard,* 1 February 1979.
68. *Morning Star,* 19 July 1979.
69. *Ibid.*
70. See, e.g. *The Guardian,* 16 July 1979.
71. *Socialist Challenge,* 13 July 1979.
72. *Morning Star,* 21 August 1979.
73. *Daily Telegraph,* 4 September 1979.
74. *Financial Times,* 13 September 1979.
75. *Hansard,* 27 November 1979, cols.1103-04.
76. *News Line,* 3 December 1979.

77. *The Times*, 7 December 1979.
78. *The Times*, 12 January 1980.
79. *The Scotsman*, 23 April 1980.
80. *The Guardian*, 24 April 1980.
81. *The Guardian*, 15 November 1980.
82. *Ibid.*
83. E.g., *The Times*, 18 November 1980; *Sunday Times*, 23 November 1980; *The Times*, 29 November 1980.
84. *Socialist Worker*, 6 December 1980.
85. *Time Out*, 7 November 1980.
86. *The Times*, 30 October 1980.
87. *Sunday Times*, 26 October 1980.
88. *Hansard*, 28 October 1980, col.214.
89. *The Guardian*, 24 October 1980.
90. *British Army Review*, December 1981.
91. *Ibid.*
92. *The Guardian*, 25 October 1980.
93. *The Times*, 27 October 1980.
94. *Hansard*, 28 October 1980, col.322.
95. *British Army Review*, December 1981.
96. *The Guardian*, 28 October 1980.
97. *British Army Review*, December 1981.
98. *Hansard*, 28 October 1980, col.216.
99. See e.g., *The Guardian*, 18 November 1980.
100. *British Army Review*, December 1981.
101. *Statement on the Defence Estimates* (1982) *op. cit.*, p.60.
102. *British Army Review*, December 1981.
103. *The Times*, 7 January 1981.
104. See e.g., *The Times*, 8 January and 25 February 1981; *The Guardian*, 7 January and 8 January 1981; *Sunday Telegraph*, 18 January 1981.
105. *The Guardian*, 14 April 1981.
106. *Sunday Telegraph*, 17 May 1981.
107. *The Times*, 30 March 1981.
108. *The Times*, 3 July 1981.
109. *The Guardian*, 23 December 1981.
110. *The Times*, 10 March 1982.
111. Statement by Baroness Young, Minister of State, DHSS. *Hansard (House of Lords)*, 5 February 1981, col.1278.
112. *Financial Times*, 17 January 1981.
113. *Ibid.* See also *The Guardian*, 17 January 1981 and *The Times*, 10 June 1981.
114. *The Times*, 20 January 1981.
115. *The Times*, 15 and 16 June 1981.
116. *The Times*, 18 June 1981.
117. *The Guardian*, 10 November 1981.
118. *Daily Telegraph*, 11 November 1981.
119. Keith Jeffery and Peter Hennessy, *States of Emergency* (1983), p.260.
120. *The Times*, 26 August 1982.
121. Jeffery and Hennessy, *op. cit.*, p.249.
122. *The Guardian*, 20 January 1983.
123. *Financial Times*, 26 January 1983.
124. *The Times*, 19 February 1983.
125. *The Guardian*, 7 April 1983.

Summary and Conclusions

The use of troops by successive governments to undermine the effectiveness of strike action has been a more extensive practice than has hitherto been realised. The use of troops for this purpose, and the way in which it has been done, raise a number of serious issues which deserve further consideration, not least by parliament and those who are most affected, trade unionists.

Military involvement in strikes is not new but the role of the troops has changed from that of maintaining order to that of a replacement work force, a role which they have been called upon to play with increasing frequency since the Second World War.

Twelve states of emergency have been declared since the Emergency Powers Act was introduced in 1920, nine of them since 1945. Troops were used on eight occasions during states of emergency. Troops have been used in 36 disputes since 1945 and government threats to send in the troops have become an increasingly frequent response to strikes in the 'essential' industries. Troops have intervened in eight dock strikes, five other disputes affecting the distribution of food, four disputes involving the production or distribution of energy, two strikes by refuse collectors, two fire brigade strikes, five disputes by civilian employees in military establishments, four health service strikes, two rail strikes and single disputes affecting the prison service, the air traffic control system, the operation of Tower Bridge and the Royal Family's hot water system.

These post-1945 military interventions fall into four broad periods: the first covers the six years 1945-51, when, with food rationed, the Labour government mobilised troops on 14 occasions, all but three of which involved food supplies. The second, more settled period, 1951-70, saw just four instances of military blacklegging, only the first of which (1953) was a major attempt at strike-breaking. The Heath government of 1970-4, the third period, was a time of considerable industrial unrest when troops were used four times, but not during the major

165

government/labour movement clashes. It is during the fourth period, from 1974 onwards, that the use of troops becomes a more common response by governments to threats to their pay and economic policies, with no less than ten instances of strike-breaking between 1977 and 1981 alone. Seven of these post-1945 military interventions were accompanied by the declaration of states of emergency under the Emergency Powers Act 1920. The 1970-4 Heath government also declared states of emergency during the two major miners strikes of 1972 and 1973-4 when troops were not actually involved.

No attempts have been made to use troops during strikes in certain industries where large numbers of skilled workers are needed, a factor often accompanied by a strong union organisation. The most prominent example of this is the coal mining industry, where even during the major miners strikes in 1972 and 1973-4 no military intervention was attempted.

The increasing frequency of the use of troops has been accompanied by the development of an extensive and sophisticated planning machinery. Civil servants constantly review the progress of disputes in the key sectors and now ensure that, where it is feasible to use troops, its network of civil administrators and the military are prepared to go into action at a moment's notice. The machinery has been reviewed and revised constantly in the light of experience.

The survey reveals that a number of factors influence the decision whether to use the troops and the timing of that decision: the fear that the presence of the troops will escalate the dispute; the extent to which to striking workers appear to have public support; the ability of the troops to carry out the work involved, depending on its complexity, the skills required and whether these are available in the forces; the degree of strain placed on the forces if the dispute is national or more than one dispute is taking place at the same time; whether the management staff remain at work and are willing to co-operate with the forces; and the extent to which the striking workers will themselves co-operate with the military, for example by allowing transportation of essential supplies.

One final factor could be a desire to familiarise the public with the idea that troops are used in this way by deploying them in low-key non-controversial disputes to make future large-scale deployment more publically acceptable. This could explain why, despite the risk of antagonising the workers on strike, governments have used troops in relatively insignificant ways in a number of disputes such as the 1970 power station manual workers dispute and the 1982 rail strike. In the latter, deployment was so minor as to go almost unnoticed by the workers involved in the dispute.

Several constitutional and legal question marks hang over the use of troops to intervene in strikes. The only time when a government clearly has the legal power to mobilise troops in strikes is when a state of emergency has been declared under the Emergency Powers Act 1920. Yet there are legal problems attached to using this legislation. The Act gives the government wide ranging powers to suspend the normal rights and liberties of citizens but emergencies can only be declared if any action is being taken that 'by interfering with the supply and distribution of food, water, fuel or light, or with the means of locomotion, [threatens] to deprive the community or any substantial portion of the community of the essentials of life.'[1] On two occasions, however, emergencies have been declared when the circumstances do not appear to have justified it: during the 1924 London tram drivers strike and during the 1966 seamens strike.

A further problem is that, during a state of emergency, the government does not have the legal authority to delegate its powers to local authorities whose employees are not civil servants. This led the government to act illegally during the General Strike and it could do so again in the future.

Governments today, however, try to avoid the drama and public interest generated when the 1920 Act is used and prefer instead to invoke what is claimed to be a residual Royal Prerogative power to deploy troops at will inside Britain, including mobilising them for strikes.

Governments may have such a power — but up until at least the First World War they did not think so. At that time it was widely accepted that, under common law, only the county magistrates, town mayors, the Metropolitan Police Commissioner and Scottish sheriffs had the authority to deploy troops within Britain. No statute since then has altered this position. As late as 1934 a War Office minister said of the government 'We do not pretend that we have any right to make use of troops in order to interfere with an industrial dispute . . .'[2] but it is not now clear whether this view reflected the law or just a popular misunderstanding of it. The Ministry of Defence now claims that it is because of the Royal Prerogative power and nothing else that it can use the troops for this purpose.

The confusion over the magistrates arises because before the First World War disturbances and strikes were synonymous, and the magistrates-based procedure which applied to disturbances was applied to strikes as well. Since the First World War strikes have not usually been accompanied by disorder, and governments have therefore claimed that the magistrates-based procedure was not relevant. For governments this is a very convenient interpretation of the law, as it removes strike interventions from local control and centralises them in a Whitehall-run administrative process, remote even from parliamentary influence. But it is by no means certain that this is legally correct. As late as 1973 the Queen's Regulations, the army's internal rule-book, defined the magistrates as the appropriate legal authorities for mobilising troops in disturbances, and it is probable that they still are today. And if the magistrates are the appropriate authorities in disturbances it is possible that they are also in strikes, as there has been no statutory reform of this area of law. Parliament or the courts should now clearly establish whether or not this is so.

Another legal question mark relating to the mobilisation of troops in industrial disputes concerns whether this sort of activity can be defined as 'military' and therefore covered by the military discipline laws. Soldiers can lawfully refuse to obey orders that are 'non-military'. Immediately after the First World War government legal advisers concluded (secretly) that strike-breaking was not 'military' and orders given to troops were therefore illegal. Nothing was done about this until 1939 when a wartime regulation (Defence Regulation Six) was passed specifically to legalise certain non-military orders. Regulation Six was continued in force by various legal measures until the Emergency Powers Act 1964 made its provisions permanent.

Illegal orders may have been given to troops involved in two recent disputes, because no Defence Council Order appears to have been made under the 1964 Act.[3] In both the 1979 incident at the Westminster Hospital and the 1977 Air Traffic Control Assistants' dispute there appears to be no official record of the 1964 Act being used (the 1977 case, however, is confused by Ministry of Defence claims that the work carried out by the troops was actually military; this is disputed by the union side).

One legal problem with the 1964 Act lies in the definition of 'urgent work of national importance' that troops can be ordered to carry out. Strikes such as that by the Glasgow Fire Brigade in 1973 can hardly be considered of 'national' importance, however urgent the local need, and it would appear that, in strikes like this, individual service personnel could lawfully refuse to obey orders.

Another difficulty is that the Act was also not intended to be used in national strikes covered by the scope of the Emergency Powers Act 1920, although this is how modern governments appear to want to use it: the most prominent example is the 1977-8 national fire brigades strike. These problems have arisen because the 1964 Act in its original form (1939 Defence Regulation Six) was specifically designed to cope with wartime production problems, particularly in agriculture.

When the contradiction between the Regulations and the 1964 Act was pointed out to the Ministry of Defence the words 'and the emergency is limited and local' were removed from the Regulations, thereby possibly laying the way open for troops to be used nationally in disputes that previously might have seen the declaration of a state of emergency.

The 1964 Act restates the government's alleged Royal Prerogative power to use troops and legalises the orders given to troops engaged in 'urgent work of national importance'. The Act is so poorly drafted that it can be read as meaning that the restatement of the Royal Prerogative power actually confers the power itself. The Act was not originally intended to do this and the Ministry of Defence does not believe it does. If it did have that meaning it would, as statute law, override the common law procedure based on magistrates: but that in turn raises political questions about the desirability of governments being able to mobilise troops in strikes without any involvement of parliament at all, as does the use of the Royal Prerogative power itself. The 1920 Act accords parliament a minimal role but the use of the Royal Prerogative power and the 1964 Act excludes parliament altogether. Whichever is the true legal basis of the government's powers to use troops, this exclusion of the democratic process should not be allowed to continue.

The official strike-breaking machine is run by civil and military contingency planners who operate largely independently of the ministers who theoretically control their work. These planners decide which strikes are potential threats and how they can be brought to an end. Military strike-breaking has developed as a covert activity, often unseen and unprotested.

The secrecy which surrounds MACM is one of its most disturbing features. Not only has the very existence of the Civil Contingencies Unit been kept secret: there are numerous examples in our survey of government decisions to keep information secret which should have been made public, as when the government realised in 1936 that regulations under the 1920 Act under which it had delegated powers to local authorities were in fact unlawful. The only reason that successive governments have got away with bending the law in this area is the excessive and totally unnecessary secrecy which surrounds it.

The government's only motive for maintaining this level of secrecy — for which there can be no grounds of national security — can only be its recognition that the use of troops to undermine strike action is a practice whose legitimacy has not been considered and accepted by the public. It is for this reason also that it insists that the troops are only there to maintain essential services, refusing to acknowledge that they also serve to reinforce government pay policies. As *The Times* noted, in the case of the 1977 Fire Brigade strike: 'At stake in this dispute, apart from the dangers to life and limb, is the future of the government's pay policy, and thereby its political credibility.'[4]

Successive governments have succeeded in blurring this distinction but it is an issue which must now be faced head on. When is it, if ever, legitimate for a government to use British troops to undermine the effectiveness of strike action?.

At one extreme, few would accept that it would be legitimate for the government to send troops into any industrial dispute. But at the other extreme, can the government sit back while public lives are at risk because the firemen, ambulance service or water workers are taking strike action? How great must the risk be to the public before it is legitimate for the government to act? These are the questions which should be debated and clarified by parliament in new legislation.

The dubious legality of the use of troops in strikes and the secrecy which surrounds government plans, has implications for another major area of policy, the maintenance of public order. The law governing the mobilisation of troops in civil disturbances is equally unclear yet the military are now fully trained for this role and the government is prepared to use them, as if there were no question of its right to do so. *The Guardian* said of the joint police-army exercise at Heathrow in 1974 that it was 'basically a public relations exercise to accustom the public to the reality of troops deploying through the high street.'[5] Certainly the announcement that the army was assisting the police at Royal Birkdale in July 1983, when the golf course had been vandalised by people protesting about the alleged wrongful conviction of a Liverpool man, Dennis Kelly, aroused no public comment let alone opposition. In the same month the army mounted a major joint exercise with the Metropolitan Police at Heathrow airport on the grounds that a terrorist attack might occur following the conviction of an Armenian terrorist. This is a separate, but related issue, deserving urgent study, before the constitutional rights of citizens are lost through lack of control over the government.

This survey and the information it has uncovered has raised more questions than it has been able to answer. It has revealed many causes for concern and pointed to issues which require further examination. At the very least it necessitates that parliament re-examine the law, clarify the conditions in which the use of troops is justified and introduce democratic procedures to be followed before their use is authorised. We hope that this book will inspire others to pursue the questions it raises and to press for these basic legislative and procedural changes.

References

1. Section 1(1).
2. *Hansard*, 11 April 1934, col.352.
3. *Hansard*, 10 July 1981, Written Answers, col.491.
4. *The Times,* 14 November 1977.
5. *The Guardian,* 8 January 1974.

Bibliography

Books, Pamphlets and Articles

Paul Addison, *The Road to 1945*, 1977.

V.I. Allen, *Trade Unions and the Government*, 1960.

A. Aspinall, *The Early English Trade Unions*, 1949.

Brian Bond, *British Military Policy between the Two World Wars*, 1980.

Sir Edwin Bramall, 'The Place of the British Army in Public Order', in *Journal of the Royal Society of Arts*, July 1980.

Tony Bunyan, *The Political Police in Britain*, 1976.

Tony Bunyan and Steve Peak, 'The British Army: 25 Years of Illegality', in *State Research Bulletin 24*, June 1981.

Angus Calder, *The People's War*, 1971.

D.G. Cattermull, 'Military Assistance to Civil Ministries — Op Burberry', in *Journal of the Royal Signals Institution*, Winter 1978.

Randolph Churchill, *Winston Churchill*, 1967.

Sir Francis de Guingand, *From Brass Hat to Bowler Hat*, 1979.

S.A. de Smith, *Constitutional and Administrative Law*, 1977.

A.V. Dicey, *Law of the Constitution*, tenth edition, 1959.

Robin Evelegh, *Peace-keeping in a Democratic Society*, 1978.

C.G. Grey, *A History of the Air Ministry*, 1940.

Halsbury's Laws of England, third and fourth editions, with supplements.

Halsbury's Statutes, fourth re-issue, 1979.

Gwyn Harries-Jenkins, 'The Collapse of the Imperial Role' in *Perspectives on British Defence Policy 1945-70*, Southampton University, 1978.

Tony Hayter, *The Army and the Crowd in Mid-Georgian England*, 1978.

Keith Jeffery and Peter Hennessy, *States of Emergency*, 1983.

Earl Jowitt and C. Walsh, *Jowitt's Dictionary of English Law*, second edition edited by John Burke, 1978.

Keesing's Contemporary Archives.

Frank Kitson, *Low Intensity Operations*, 1971.

K.G.J.C. Knowles, *Strikes: A Study in Industrial Conflict*, 1952.

Labour Government versus the Dockers 1945-51, Solidarity Pamphlet 19, second edition, 1966.

Robert Mark, *Policing a Perplexed Society*, 1977.

Geoffrey Marshall, 'The Armed Forces and Industrial Disputes in the United Kingdom', in *Armed Forces and Society*, February 1979.

Esther Moir, *The Justice of the Peace*, 1969.

Lord Moran, *Winston Churchill: The Struggle for Survival 1940-1965*, 1966.

A.L. Morton, *A People's History of England*, 1965.

Gillian S. Morris, 'The Emergency Powers Act 1920' in *Public Law*, Winter 1969; and 'The Police and Industrial Emergencies' in *Industrial Law Journal*, March 1980.

Margaret Morris, *The General Strike*, 1976.

Henry Pelling, *A History of British Trade Unionism*, 1971.

K. Perkins, 'Soldiers or Policemen?', in *British Army Review*, 1973.

O. Hood Phillips, *Constitutional and Administrative Law*, fifth edition, 1973.

L. Radzinowicz, *A History of English Criminal Law, volume four: Grappling for Control*, 1968.

Robert Rizzi, 'The British Army and Riot Control in Early Nineteenth Century England' in *Army Quarterly*, January 1979.

Royal United Services Institute, *Internal Security — a Neglected Aspect of Defence*, speeches given at a RUSI seminar, 1976.

Philip Schlesinger, 'On the Shape and Scope of Counter-Insurgency Thought' in *Power and the State*, edited by G. Littlejohn, 1978.

Brian Sedgemore, *The Secret Constitution*, 1978.

Alan Sked and Chris Cook, *Post-War Britain*, 1979.

J.C. Smith and B. Hogan, *Criminal Law*, fourth edition, 1978.

Michael Supperstone, *Brownlie's Law of Public Order and National Security*, second edition, 1981.

O. Teichman, 'The Yeomanry as an Aid to Civil Power, 1795-1867' in *Journal of the Society for Army Historical Research*, 1940.

Tony Topham, 'The Attack on the Dockers', in *Trade Union Register Three*, edited by Michael Barratt Brown and Ken Coates, 1973.

C.H. Van der Noot, 'The Soldier's Lot . . . Prison Warder — Fireman', in *British Army Review*, 1981.

E.C.S. Wade and G. Godfrey Phillips, *Constitutional and Administrative Law*, ninth edition by A.W. Bradley, 1977.

Sidney and Beatrice Webb, *The History of Trade Unionism*, 1920.

Christopher J. Whelan, 'Military Intervention in Industrial Disputes' in *Industrial Law Journal*, December 1979; and 'The Law and the Use of Troops in Industrial Disputes' in *Law, State and Society*, edited by Bob Fryer *et al.*, 1981.

Harold Wilson, *The Labour Government 1964-70*, 1971.

Official Publications

Hansard Record of Parliamentary Debates.

Public Record Office documents.

Queen's Regulations for the Army, various editions to date.

Manual of Military Law, various editions to date.

Report of the Committee of Inquiry into the Disturbances at Featherstone, 1893, Parliamentary Papers.

Report of the Select Committee on the Employment of the Military in Cases of Disturbances, 1908, Parliamentary Papers.

Review of the British Docks Strikes 1949, 1949, Parliamentary Papers.

Report of the Committee of Inquiry into Stoppages in the London Docks, Ministry of Labour, 1951, Parliamentary Papers.

Annual *Statements on the Defence Estimates* (also known as the Defence White Papers).

Army Training Manual of Land Operations, particularly volume one: *The Fundamentals* and volume three: *Counter Revolutionary Operations*, revised to 1973.

British Labour Statistics: Historical Abstract 1886-1968, Department of Employment, 1971.

Periodicals

Daily newspapers, particularly *The Times, The Guardian, Daily Telegraph, Morning Star* (and its predecessor the *Daily Worker*) and *News Line* (and its predecessor the *Workers' Press*).

Magazines such as *The Leveller, Socialist Worker, Socialist Challenge, The Economist,* and *The Listener.*

Specialist journals, particularly the *State Research Bulletin, Army Quarterly, British Army Review,* the official journals of the various units of the armed forces, *Royal United Services Institute Journal,* trade union journals, annual reports of the TUC, *Industrial Law Journal, Public Law* and *Armed Forces and Society.*

Index

Name Index

Subject Index

The Cobden Trust

The Cobden Trust is a registered charity established in 1963 to undertake research and education work in the field of civil liberties. It seeks the protection and extension of civil liberties in the United Kingdom and has a two fold strategy to achieve this: research, into the causes of injustice, and education work, informing the public about their rights and responsibilities.

How can you help

While we are able to raise funds from charitable trusts and foundations, we depend also on generous public support. As a registered charity, the Trust can recover tax from the Inland Revenue on any covenanted donation. If you would like to help us in this way, or would like further information, then please write for details to the Secretary, the Cobden Trust, 21 Tabard Street, London SE1 4LA.